Pocketful of Puppets:

Mother Goose
By Tamara Hunt and Nancy Renfro

Nancy Renfro Studios
Austin, Texas

Other Books published by Nancy Renfro Studios
Puppetry in Education Series

PUPPET CORNER IN EVERY LIBRARY
PUPPETRY AND THE ART OF STORY CREATION
PUPPETRY AND CREATIVE DRAMATICS IN STORYTELLING
PUPPETRY AND EARLY CHILDHOOD EDUCATION
MAKE AMAZING PUPPETS (Learning Works)
POCKETFUL OF PUPPETS (Series)

(Can be obtained from address below)

ISBN 0-931044-06-5

Published in the United States of America by
Nancy Renfro Studios 1117 W. 9th Street, Austin Texas 78703

Photographs by Tamara Hunt and Amos Dague
Illustrations by Nancy Renfro

For Tara Melia
*who has sparkle in her eyes
and magic in her laughter*

The Teachers

Susana Afaya Bowman
Lorilei Hirota
Annette Hoffman
Vicky K. Iwaki
Joel Light

ACKNOWLEDGMENTS

This book owes its existence to my husband John: who, night after night read Mother Goose to our four year old daughter Tara as part of her bedtime stories. As I sat in the living room listening to them singing and laughing their way through the rhymes, I began to re-discover the rhythm and humor that appeals so wondrously to young children. And because Tara took them all to heart, memorizing and reciting them with dramatic flair and non-sensical pleasure, it seemed fitting that this book should be dedicated to her. It is to both Tara and John that I extend my greatest appreciation.

A special thanks also goes to my seven year old son Ian who is my greatest fan and in so being, encourages me in the search for new ideas and approaches to puppetry.

The book could not have been completed without the assistance of the teachers at the Family Learning Center in Honolulu, Hawaii, Susana Afaga Bowman, Gail Hayashi and Lee-Ann Miyasaki who allowed me to "adopt" their schools and photograph the children engaged in puppetry activities.

And of course I am most fortunate to have as collaborator Nancy Renfro, who likes my ideas, gives strength to my weaknesses and makes writing a reality and a joy!

Dr. Tamara Hunt
Professor of Theatre
University of Hawaii
Honolulu, Hawaii

I do not recall having been read nursery rhymes as a child, and having no children of my own, I had no opportunity to relive them as an adult. Thus, the happy occasion of working on this Mother Goose book with Tammy has given me childhood refound. Because I am a visual person—due to a hearing impairment—the rhymes have taken on special meaning and coloration as they are brought to life through puppets. Now I delight in searching through Mother Goose's pockets and discovering her endless repertoire of verses.

Many thanks to Debbie Sullivan who assisted us with her artistic talents in creating many of the puppets in this book.

Also, to Ann Weiss Schwalb for her continual faith in our work at the Studios and role as advisor, consultant, and editor.

And to Tammy Hunt who introduced me to the magic of Mother Goose!

Nancy Renfro

TABLE OF CONTENTS

The Poor Dog in Old Mother Hubbard

INTRODUCTION

As children we joyfully sang, frolicked, and giggled our way through Mother Goose rhymes. It seemed that no matter how many times we heard these same rhymes, we never tired of listening to their poesy measure and bantering lyrics. The introduction of computers, science fiction, and modern technology has done nothing to diminish the appeal of Mother Goose. These rhymes endure faithfully in a state of timelessness which will continue to enrich the lives of children for many generations to come.

Mother Goose offers a unique opportunity for sharing to take place between children and their parents, their teachers, and the other special adults in their lives. This book attempts to strengthen the bond by introducing a new wrinkle to the process: the merging of puppets with Mother Goose rhymes. Humpty Dumpty, Little Miss Muffet, and Old King Cole, with the advent of puppets, come vibrantly to life. So fill your pockets with puppets, harness the Gander, and come join us as we frolic our way through the World of Mother Goose!

USING THE BOOK

Each rhyme in this book is arranged in such a way as to present the simplest activity first, with varying supplemental activities following.

The basic format is as follows:

Introducing the Rhyme — Stimulate interest by asking direct questions that relate to each rhyme, questions of a thematic or a specific nature. For example, in "Little Bo Peep" the verse revolves around the subject of a lost animal, providing an excellent opportunity to discuss the concept of being lost, with the children. "What would you do if you were Little Bo Peep?" "Where would you look?" "How would you feel if you got lost?" Each rhyme has its own focus which can be expanded as a point of further discussion or to more effectively personalize the rhyme for the child.

Puppetelling — In Puppetelling, the leader is a storyteller using puppets informally, either over the lap or in an open space, rather than in the formal setting of the stage. The storyteller simply recites the rhymes, using the puppets for visual focus. Group the children, when possible, in an informal semi-circle, so that they may easily share in the experience. They may even be asked to manipulate the puppets themselves when there are too many characters for the leader to handle.

Always keep your puppets moving with vitality and purpose. Have fun experimenting with voices, gestures, and expressions. Try using a deep resonant voice for the Sheep in "Baa, Baa, Black Sheep," and a high squeaky voice for the Pussycat in "Pussycat, Pussycat, Where Have You Been?" Strive for variety in voice.

The leader might even consider "becoming" Mother Goose, dressed in a costume or apron, and talking with a crackly, old woman's voice; one's natural voice is also acceptable. On the other hand, if you prefer to use a Goose or Old Woman puppet, then practice using the puppet with an appropriate voice for Mother Goose. It might be fun to have an Old Woman puppet flying in on a Gander's back at the beginning of the storytelling session and then fly away again at the conclusion.

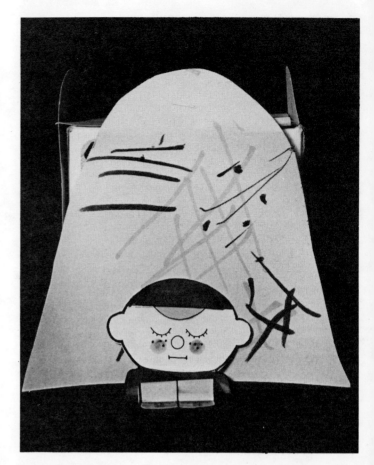

Little Boy Blue

Consider integrating simple props, sound, and special effects to embellish your presentation. Realia is quite effective in certain circumstances; for example, use a real shoe or high boot for "There Was An Old Woman Who Lived in a Shoe" or, a candle stick for "Jack Be Nimble." The children might provide clucking sounds for "My Black Hen" as she lays her precious eggs or tick-tock sound effects for "Hickory, Dickory, Dock." Or, a child could hold a gong for striking when "The Clock Struck One." Keep a boxful of musical instruments and other noisemakers on hand, for adding audial, as well as visual stimulation to the experience.

Puppetmaking —Each rhyme has simple puppetmaking activities accompanying it with a list of required materials and easy procedures for construction. In many cases, patterns are provided for individual classroom duplication. The puppets shown for each activity is generally the same type used by both the leader in the Puppetelling activity and the children in the Puppetizing activity.

Although patterns are provided throughout this book it is important for the children to have as many creative Puppetmaking experiences as possible, without the use of patterns. The primary purpose for inclusion of the patterns is to aid the leader, who may wish to use them, or when time is a limiting factor. The leader may wish to improvise his or her own ideas for the Puppetmaking session in order to enhance the experience. In "Sing a Song of Sixpence," the children can create their own paper Blackbirds to affix onto finger tubes rather than use the pattern in the book. Or, large cut-out paper Blackbirds can be attached to rod controls for a completely different effect.

Every Puppetmaking activity also includes a special materials list of key materials required to do that particular project. These vary from activity to activity.

In addition have on hand some of the following basic materials for puppetmaking activities:

Brushes — small, medium, large sizes
Cardboard — posterboard, oak-tag
Coloring Media — pencils, crayons,
    felt-tipped marker pens, tempera paint
Construction Paper — assorted colors
Fabrics — assorted textures and types
Felt — many colors
Glue — white glue, glue sticks, rubber
    cement, paste
Scissors — blunt tipped
Stapler — desk and hand types
Tape — masking cellophane

Puppetizing — Puppetizing is a dramatization of the rhyme by the children using puppets; it can involve pantomime or voice, but it is always on an improvisational level. Creative dramatics is the central process in Puppetizing and the children are given opportunity to repeat the rhyme on a wider level with deeper involvement than through the initial Puppetelling.

When puppets are completed, gather the children with their puppets around the playing circle to discuss the parts in the rhyme and to assign roles. Cue the children on what each character will say or do, and block out the scene and actions as a group. Be very clear in designating specific locations or landmarks in the playing circle such as hill, tree, or house. Landmarks can be imagined altogether or designated by such things as chairs, tables, and rugs.

After Puppetizing the activity, discuss with the children in positive, supportive ways, all the things you like about their presentation. Encourage the children to suggest new ideas for next time, and then recast the characters, giving other children a chance to play the roles for as long as interest level remains high.

As you gain experience and expertise, you may eventually venture out and try your own combinations of puppets and rhymes. Many of the puppet types are interchangeable with various verses. For example, the Paper-Plate Masks in "Hey Diddle Diddle" are perfectly suited puppet types to use for the lead characters in "Jack and Jill" or, as sheep in "Baa, Baa, Black Sheep." The Envelope Puppets in "One to Ten" would also be an excellent kind of puppet to use for playing the royal characters in "Sing a Song of Sixpence."

The puppet world of Mother Goose is a multi-dimensional world. As soon as you try one level and see the delight reflected in the children's eyes, you will find yourself seeking that delight on other levels which you and the children can invent together.

Apron designed by Annette Hoffman   Flower Puppet by Nancy Renfro Studios

PRESENTATION IDEAS

You might wish to consider adding a few basic items to liven up and add interest to your Mother Goose collection of rhymes.

STORY APRON

A Story Apron: A colorful Story Apron with oversized pockets is perfect for concealing puppets, props, and other surprises. Children will delight in seeing tails, dangling feet, and eyes peering over the tops of the pockets. The Story Apron also signals to them that a story session is about to begin with some special fun in store. You might wish to take on the role of Mother Goose with appropriate apron and costuming. Fabric shops often carry patterns for constructing a ruffled apron of your own. Or consider purchasing a ready made one at a department store. A frilly hat or bonnet is a nice touch. An older rendition of Mother Goose can be achieved with a white wig and granny glasses. If you prefer a simpler setup, then a plain butcher style apron with pockets as shown with *Bat, Bat, Come Under My Hat* will serve nicely.

A Lapboard: This simple board is used primarily as a "stage" for putting on your lap and resting a book or standing up puppets or props. Simply cover a rectangle of 12 inch by 18 inch cardboard with a piece of felt or contact paper.

Although each rhyme in this book is accompanied by specific ideas of puppetmaking and related activities, the storyteller may wish to venture off and try other presentation forms. The following are some suggestions based on specific techniques:

STORY GLOVES

Story gloves complement finger plays. Almost all gloves work well and interchangeability can be achieved with a basic glove.

Rubber Household Glove — Provides a smooth surface for adhering small picture images such as drawings, photographs, greeting cards, or magazine pictures. Cut out image and laminate with clear contact paper or plastic laminate for permanency, if desired. Put a piece of double-stick tape on the back of each image and secure to tips of glove.

Garden Glove — Garden gloves come in an interesting variety of designs and colors while making a sturdy glove for all around use. Sew small pieces of velcro to tips of glove. Make characters from drapery pom-poms and glue corresponding pieces of velcro to the backs of pom-poms for attaching to glove. Changing felt scenery such as a clock, moon, or palace can be attached to the palm area of glove by means of velcro or a button.

Pellon Glove — Make basic glove from heavyweight Pellon (interlining fabric) using pattern that follows. Use marker pens to color a scenic background, such as a garden, mountain, pond or starlit sky. Paper images can be attached to the glove tips by means of paper clips. Open up the paper clip slightly, and glue or tape to back of image. Cut a crosswise slit on each glove tip about 1/3 inch down to insert the paper clip through.

There was an Old Woman

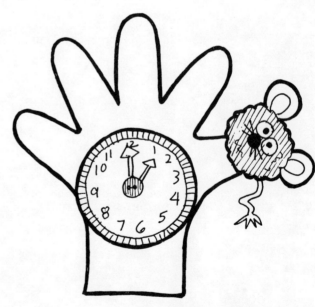

Hickory, Dickory Dock

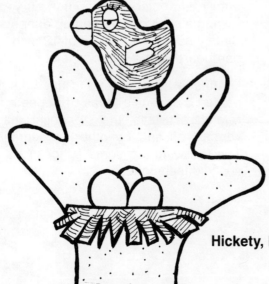

Hickety, Pickety, My Black Hen

16

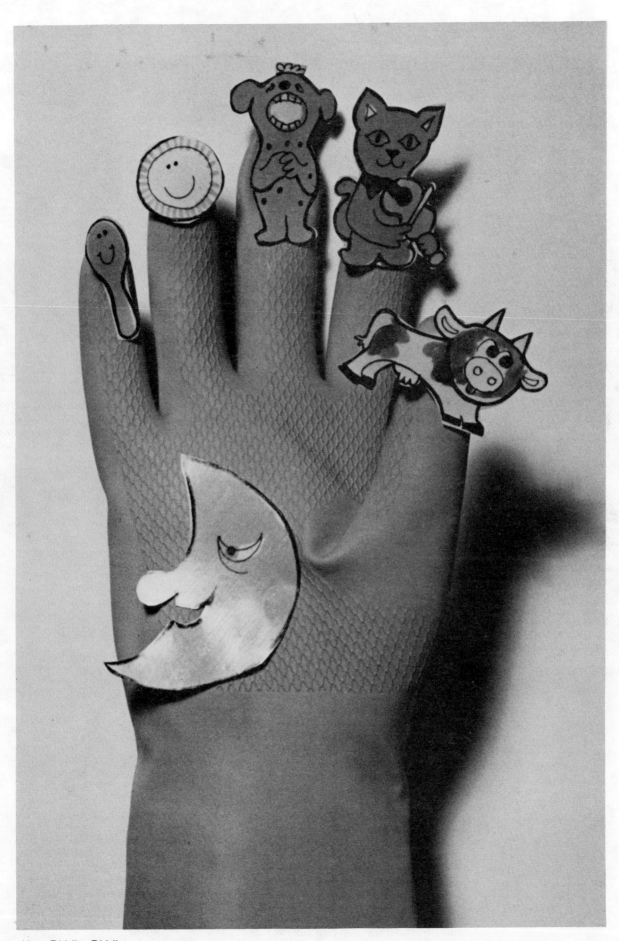

Hey, Diddle, Diddle

GLOVE PATTERN

CUP AND
CONTAINER THEATERS

Individualized theaters made from paper cups or cut down food boxes are intriguing visuals to depict nursery rhymes. Children can make their own mobile theater to aid in dramatizing the rhyme. Once completed, theaters can be brought home as a memory of the puppet experience. Tape a small drawing or picture (magazine, greeting card, or other) to end of a drinking straw; slip other end of straw through hole punctured in bottom of container. Attach scenic suggestions to edge of container and decorate exterior to match story theme.

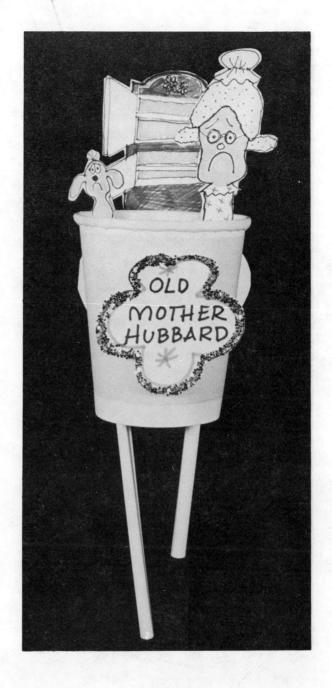

The Man in the Moon

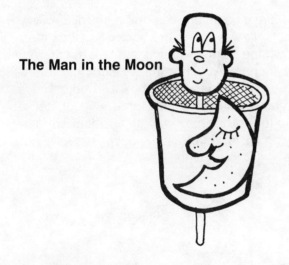

Two Birds

Humpty Dumpty

Mary, Mary, Quite Contrary

BOOK THEATERS

A storybook itself may provide a natural theater with the front and back covers as well as interior illustrations furnishing background scenery for Puppetelling. Mother Goose can ride her gander, Jack jump over the candlestick or Little Bo Peep go search for her sheep over the top edge of the book. Place the book on a table with the outside covers facing the children. This positioning will allow the Puppeteller to read the inside text while gliding the puppets along the top edge of the book.

Puppets can be made from paper cut-outs glued to drinking straws or popsicle sticks. Scenery and props, attached to spring clothespins, may be secured to the top of the book. If you are familiar enough with the story so that the text does not have to be read, then turn the pages of the book toward the children, thus allowing each page to create a different scene. Fingerpuppets are excellent for use with Book Theaters.

Jack Be Nimble

THEATERS-TO-WEAR

Children love to take turns trying on this novel theater to tell their own versions of rhymes. It also provides an excellent theater for the teacher to Puppetell. A Theater-To-Wear can be attached around the neck and hung within easy reach in front of the standing Puppeteller. Fingerpuppets and small rod puppets are particularly well-suited for dramatizations. The advantage of this theater is that many characters can be maneuvered at one time with the use of rods. Rod puppets on very thin dowels or drinking straws can be made to adhere to double-backed carpeting tape that has been affixed to the front inside edge of a cut-down box. Several rod puppets that have already been introduced early in the story can remain in position while other puppets are brought into play.

To make a basic theater, find a sturdy grocery carton. Cut away the entire back of the box then cut down the front and ends to a height of ten to twelve inches. Attach a heavy cord or ribbon length to both sides of the box and adjust to a comfortable fit for hanging around your neck. The bottom of the box makes an ideal surface for laying a storybook or puppets presently not in use.

neck tie

I Saw a Ship A-Sailing

The Rhymes

BAA, BAA, BLACK SHEEP

Baa, baa, black sheep,
Have you any wool?
Yes merry have I,
Three bags full;

One for my master,
One for my dame,
And one for the little boy
Who lives in the lane.

Introducing the Rhyme: Ask the children to think of all the things that keep them warm such as sweaters, blankets, and coats. Talk about wool and where it comes from. Have the children check to see if anyone is wearing wool.

Puppetelling: Place three small paper or cloth bags on a lapboard or table. Introduce your Black Sheep Envelope Puppet to the children and recite the poem, using a contrasting voice for the Sheep's part. Fill each bag with a piece of wool taken from the Sheep's body at the appropriate times in the rhyme.

Puppetmaking: Let each child make a Black Sheep Envelope Puppet for giving wool.

Materials — 6½ x 3½ inch envelope; construction paper; and cotton balls or polyester fiber.

Construction — To make head, tuck in the flap of the envelope. Put hand inside envelope as shown. Gently "bite" finger of other hand to form puppet's mouth; straighten out mouth if wrinkled. Attach a paper body and ears to envelope head. Draw in features or add paper ones. Add cotton balls. They can be made removable by tucking them into small holes cut into the paper body of the Sheep, or by using double-backed tape.

Puppetizing: Invite the children, one by one, to come up to your lapboard and play the part of the Sheep. Let each new puppeteer select three children from the group to be the Master, the Dame, and the Little Boy, without puppets, and give the wool to them as the rhyme is recited. Children who are seated around the playing circle can ask the initial question: "Baa, baa, black sheep, have you any wool?" The child whose turn it is to play the Sheep can respond by reciting the remainder of the rhyme. Afterwards, ask the three characters what they plan to do with their bags of wool.

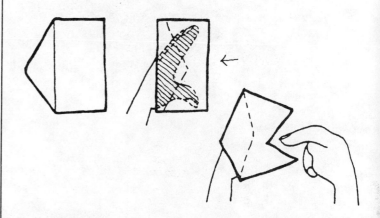

paper

Sheep Envelope Puppet

cotton

paper body

paper bags

23

24

BAT, BAT, COME UNDER MY HAT

Bat, bat, come under my hat,
And I will give you a slice of bacon,
And when I bake,
I'll give you a cake,
If I am not mistaken.

Introducing the Rhyme: Ask the children, "If you could play a trick on someone and hide something under your hat, what would it be?" Put a hat on your head and ask, "What do you suppose I'm going to hide under my hat?"

Puppetelling: Hide the Bat in your puppet apron and call it to come out at the beginning of the rhyme. Give it a shy personality and try to teasingly entice it to come out with the promise of bacon and cake. At the end of the rhyme, the Bat can fly up and under your hat!

Puppetmaking: Ask each child to make a fancy hat and Bat Finger Puppet to hide under the hat.

Materials — Photocopy of Bat pattern; and small rubber band.

Construction — Cut out and color Bat. Staple the rubber band across back of Bat as shown for inserting finger.

To Make Paper-Bag Hat — Slit a small or medium-sized paper bag, half way up, at all four corners. Fold out the four side flaps and crease. Decorate with fancy magazine pictures of flowers, bugs, etc., ribbons, sequins, scrap fabrics and other materials.

Puppetizing: Invite the children to recite the rhyme as they tuck the Bat Puppets under their hats. Increase the learning experience for the children by changing the rhyme so that the Bat flies *over, above, around, to the left of, to the right of, faraway from,* and *close to* the hat. You also can have the Bat hide under various body parts such as arm, hand, foot, leg, and chin.

Paper Bag Hat

rubber band

BAT PATTERN

25

CACKLE, CACKLE, MOTHER GOOSE

Cackle, cackle, Mother Goose,
Have you any feathers loose?
Truly have I, pretty fellow,
Half enough to fill a pillow.
And here are quills, take one or ten,
And make from each, a little pen.

Introducing the Rhyme: Talk about goose feathers and how the small soft feathers are used to make pillows and quilts and the large, stiff feathers quills. If possible bring in some real feathers for the children to see and touch. Show the children what a quill is by turning a feather into a pen and writing with it dipped in ink or thin paint.

Puppetelling: Introduce your Mother Goose Box Puppet to the children. Point out to them that she doesn't have any quills. Explain to the children that before you can tell them the rhyme, everyone will have to help by making quills for Mother Goose to wear.

Invite the children to the playing circle and introduce the Mother Goose Puppet. Comment on how beautiful she looks with her new feathers. Say the rhyme using a cackly, funny voice for Mother Goose. At the end of the rhyme let the children come up one by one and take out their quills. Ask each child to tell Mother Goose what they plan to do with their quills. Perhaps Mother Goose could grant each child a wish before they take the feathers home.

Puppetmaking: Have the children make a paper quill. Encourage them to create their own designs and colors (This is a very "fancy" Mother Goose and her feathers need not be all white). They may even want to write their names or draw faces on their quills!

Materials — White paper; and plastic drinking straw.

Construction — Cut out a quill shape from white paper and glue or tape a drinking straw down the center back. Fringe edges of quill with scissors to create a "feathered"

look and then decorate it.

To Make Mother Goose Puppet:

Materials — Cereal, detergent, or other box for body; cardboard towel tube for neck; white paper; and fabric for bonnet.

Construction — Cover box and cardboard neck tube completely with white paper. Cut a circle in the top of the box for inserting the neck tube into and glue in place. Add a white paper head with beak, eyes, and bonnet to top of neck tube. Attach paper wings to sides of box and puncture small holes all over the box for inserting quills.

Puppetizing: Expand the activity through creative drama by asking the children to become Mother Goose exploring her movements with their bodies. "How does she hold up her neck?" "How does she walk and shake her feathers about?" "How does she feel about her beautiful feathers?" Have the children parade around the room as Mother Goose.

Quill

26

THE CAT AND THE FIDDLE

Hey, diddle, diddle!
The cat and the fiddle,
The cow jumped over the moon;
The little dog laughed,
To see such sport,
And the dish ran away with the spoon!

Introducing the Rhyme: Ask the children what the word "nonsense" means. "What is the silliest thing you can think of?" "Have *you* ever done anything silly?"

Puppetelling: Use Paper-Plate Puppets of the characters. Tuck them away in your apron pockets or lay them face down on a lapboard. Recite the rhyme showing each character at the appropriate time.

Puppetmaking: Ask each child to make a Paper-Plate Puppet of one of the characters in the rhyme.

Materials — Paper plate; blunt skewer, cardboard towel tube, or stick for rod control; and construction paper.

Construction — Tape the rod control onto the back of the paper plate. Use coloring medium or paper for making features. Cut out eye holes for converting puppets into masks, if desired.

Puppetizing: Before puppetizing the rhyme, let the children practice becoming the different characters, exploring voices and body movements for a meowing cat, jumping cow, laughing dog, flat round dish, tall straight spoon, and a fiddle. When everyone has had a turn, select the puppeteers to act out the poem with their puppets.

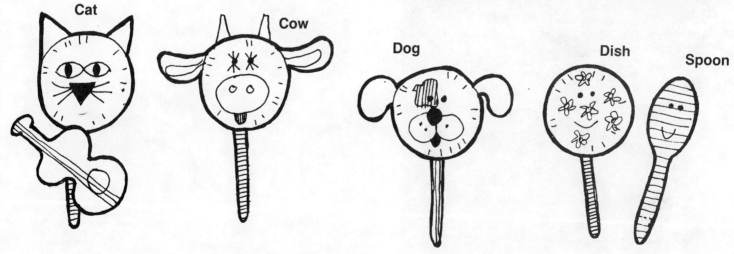

Cat   Cow   Dog   Dish   Spoon

DANCE, THUMBKIN, DANCE

Dance, Thumbkin, dance;
Dance, ye merrymen, everyone:
For Thumbkin, he can dance alone,
Thumbkin, he can dance alone.

Dance, Foreman, Dance,
Dance, ye merrymen, everone:
But Foreman, he can dance alone,
Foreman, he can dance alone.

Dance Longman, dance,
Dance, ye merrymen, everyone:
For Longman, he can dance alone,
Longman, he can dance alone.

Dance, Ringman, dance,
Dance, ye merrymen, everyone:
But Ringman can dance alone,
Ringman, he can dance alone.

Dance, Littleman, dance,
Dance, ye merrymen, everyone:
But Littleman, he can dance alone,
Littleman, he can dance alone.

Introducing the Rhyme: Have the children hold up each appropriate finger as they identify it. Then ask, "What can you do with your different fingers?" (such as point, eat, lick and turn pages).

Then have the children mime some of the following finger activities:

- Point in different directions
- Lick a cake bowl
- Eat a cookie
- Make a circle in the sand
- Pick up a bug
- Finger paint

Puppetelling: Using Circle Finger Puppets, act out the rhyme for the children. Encourage them to join in following your actions using their bare fingers.

Puppetmaking: Ask the children to make their own Circle Finger Puppets for dancing. Double-backed tape can be used for attaching the circles to the children's fingers.

Materials — Photocopy of circle face patterns; and double-backed tape.

Construction — Cut out and color circle in different colors.

Puppetizing: Invite the children back to the playing circle where everyone can participate in the rhyme using their Circle Puppets.

Ask the children to think up other simple activities to do with their Finger Puppets, such as:

- Thumbkin goes around in circles.
- Foreman jumps over a toy.
- Longman lies down to sleep.
- Ringman sings a song.
- Littleman gives the leader a kiss.

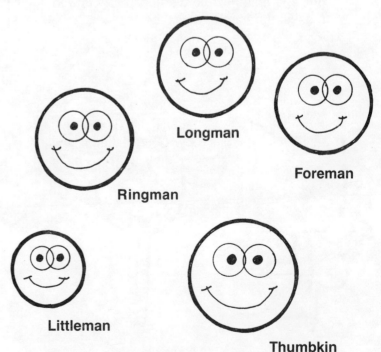

Longman

Foreman

Ringman

Littleman

Thumbkin

DANCE TO YOUR DADDY

Dance to your daddy,
My little baby,
Dance to your daddy, my little lamb!
You shall have a fishy,
In a little dishy,
You shall have a fishy when the boat comes in.

Dance to your daddy,
My little baby,
Dance to your daddy, my little lamb!
You shall have an apple,
You shall have a plum,
You shall have a rattle,
When your daddy comes home.

Introducing the Rhyme: Ask the children if they like to dance. Have they ever danced for their mother or father before?

Puppetelling: Introduce the Little Baby Finger Puppet to the children and recite the rhyme as you make the Baby dance following the actions of the rhyme. Use paper or real props (fish, dish, boat, apple, plum and rattle) and pull out from a hiding place, one by one, as you incorporate them into the action.

BABY PATTERN

Puppetmaking: Let each child make a Little Baby Finger Puppet to join in a dance activity.

Materials — Photocopy of pattern; coloring medium; and small rubber band.

Construction· — Cut out and color Baby pattern. Staple rubber band across back of puppet and insert first and second finger through for "dancing legs."

To Make Paper Props — Cut out and color the patterns. Reinforce by gluing onto stiff paper.

Puppetizing: Ask the children to gather around a table and use the table surface to dance their puppets on. Play some lively music, if desired, and recite the poem as all the children make their puppets dance together. You may distribute the various paper props to different children as the rhyme is recited. A Mother character can be alternately substituted for Daddy if desired.

Afterwards, have the children form a cradle with one hand and place their Little Baby puppet in the cradle to sleep. Have them rock their hands back and forth as you recite the following well-loved rhyme:

Hush a bye, baby, on the tree top,
When the wind blows the cradle will rock;
When the bough breaks the cradle will fall,
Down will come baby, cradle, and all.

rubber band

fingers

FIVE LITTLE PIGS

This little pig went to market;
This little pig stayed home;
This little pig had roast beef;
This little pig had none;
This little pig said, "Wee, wee!
I can't find my way home."

Introducing the Rhyme: Ask the children if their mother or father has ever played the Five Little Pigs on their toes before. "What did you like best about that game?" "What would you buy if you were the first Little Pig that went to market?" "What would you do if you stayed home?" "What could be your favorite food to eat?" Introduce your Five Little Pigs Finger Puppets.

Puppetelling: Recite the rhyme using a rubber household or other glove for sticking on the Pig Finger Puppets. Fold each Little Pig down at the appropriate time. At the end of the rhyme, the only one showing should be the Little Pig.

Puppetmaking: Ask each child to make a Little Pig Finger Puppet to use to find their way home.

Materials — Photocopy of Little Pig pattern; and double-stick tape.

Construction — Color and cut out the Little Pig pattern. Put a piece of double-stick tape on the back and attach to child's finger.

To Make Other Pigs — Follow the same instructions as above.

Puppetizing: Invite the children back to the playing circle. Ask several of the children to stand in the middle and form one big house with their bodies. Select another child to be the Little Pig and hide somewhere in the room. All the children can say the rhyme together, and at the end, the Little Pig puppeteer can make crying sounds while trying to find its way home while going inside the house.

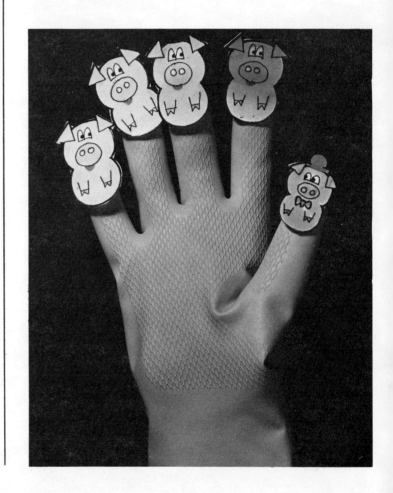

FIVE PIG PATTERNS

30

HICKETY, PICKETY, MY BLACK HEN

Hickety, pickety, my black hen,
She lays eggs for gentlemen;
Gentlemen come every day,
To see what my black hen doth lay.

Introducing the Rhyme: Ask the children, "Who had eggs for breakfast?" "How do you like your eggs cooked?" "What tasty things can be made from eggs?" (cakes, cookies, bread, etc.) "Where do you suppose eggs come from?"

Puppetelling: Have the children imagine that they are Gentlemen who have come to visit your farm. Ask, "Would you like to meet my Black Hen?" Then bring out your Black Hen Box Puppet and nest with eggs. Hide the eggs inside the Hen's special cardboard tube egg holder. Recite the rhyme and lift the Hen up at the end to reveal a plastic or hardboiled egg underneath. This is an excellent Easter activity to do with decorated eggs.

Puppetmaking: Let the children make their own miniature laying Hen Tube Puppets with jelly bean eggs to lay eggs.

Hen Tube Puppet

Materials — Short cardboard tube; construction paper; jelly beans; and real or paper feathers.

Construction — Cut out and color a picture of a Hen from construction paper and glue to one side of tube. Attach a feather to top of head or back of tube for tail. Put some jelly beans under hen for hatching. Make miniature nests from jar lids or small paper soup bowls. Some dried grass or fringed paper would make the nest more authentic.

Hen Box Puppet

Materials — Salt or oatmeal box; cardboard; construction paper or felt features; and red shag fur, paper, or real feathers.

Construction — Remove lid from oatmeal box or cut off end of salt box; turn upside down. Cut out two opposite side shapes from cardboard for Hen's body, large enough to cover the box area. Add a cardboard or felt beak and other features. Hen's body can be decorated by covering with red shag fur, fringed tissue paper, or real or paper feathers. To make an egg holder for Hen, roll up a piece of cardboard into a tube shape, large enough for slipping in several eggs. Tape the tube inside box and place eggs up tube. Hen can then lay one egg at a time, by lifting up the body.

To Make Nest — Curve a 2 inch wide strip of cardboard into a 7 inch diameter circle and staple ends together. Glue circular strip down onto a lightweight cardboard circle of a corresponding size and let dry. Glue straw or fringed paper onto outer surface of nest. Place Hen on nest with eggs hidden underneath her.

Puppetizing: The children can take turns reciting the rhyme with their Hen puppets and surprise the other children with their jelly bean eggs underneath. (They may wish to share the eggs with the group afterwards.)

For a creative dramatics activity, the children can pretend to be the Hens, making clucking sounds, while sitting on pillows or rugs as the rhyme is recited. The leader can play the role of a Gentleman while walking around the playing circle and buying or collecting imaginary eggs.

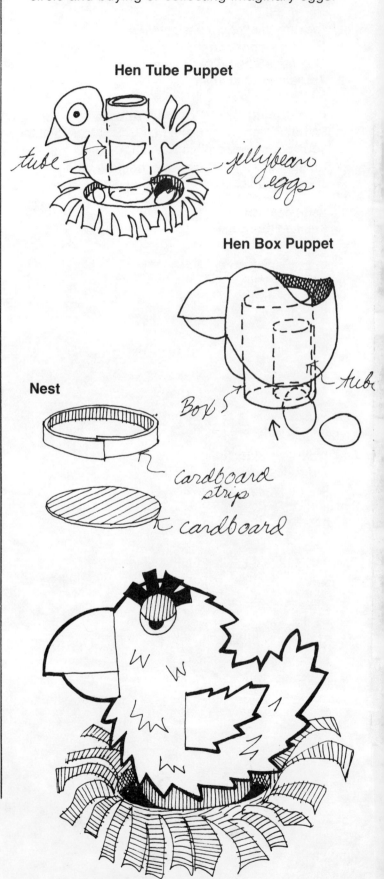

Hen Tube Puppet

Hen Box Puppet

Nest

HICKORY, DICKORY DOCK

Hickory, dickory, dock!
The mouse ran up the clock;
The clock struck one,
And down he'd come,
Hickory, dickory, dock!

Introducing the Rhyme: Show the children your Paper-Plate Clock. Ask them to identify the numbers on the Clock. Talk about what the children do at special times during the day.

Puppetelling: Place the Clock around your neck and show it to the children. Ask them to find the One O'Clock digit on its face. Introduce the Mouse Finger Puppet to the children. Stand up and recite the rhyme as your Mouse runs up and down the Clock. Change the arms on your Clock to a different time. Repeat the poem, substituting the new time. Do not be concerned if the numbers do not rhyme within the verse.

Puppetmaking: Have each child create a Mouse Finger Puppet to help in telling time.

Materials — Photocopy of Mouse pattern; and coloring medium.

Construction — Cut out and color the Mouse pattern. Bend tabs into a tube shape to fit finger and glue together.

To Make Clock — Cut out two paper hands. Attach the center of a paper plate with paper fastener. Mark numbers on Clock. Staple a length of ribbon to top and tie around neck.

Puppetizing: Gather the children around the playing circle. Invite them one at a time to make their Mouse run up and down your Clock. Let each child select a new time on the Clock for the Mouse.

Expand the activity by letting each Mouse find something else in the room to run up and down when the Clock strikes one. (A door, another child, a toy structure, etc.).

bend tab into curve

MOUSE PATTERN

I SAW A SHIP A-SAILING

I saw a ship a-sailing,
A-sailing on the sea;
And, oh! It was all laden,
With pretty things for thee.

There were comfits in the cabin,
And apples in the hold;
The sails were made of silk,
And the masts were made of gold.

The four-and-twenty sailors,
That stood between the decks;
Were four-and-twenty white mice,
With chains about their necks.

The captain was a duck,
With a packet on his back;
And when the ship began to move,
The captain said, "Quack! Quack!"

Introducing the Rhyme: Ask the children, "Have they ever been on a boat ride before?" "Was it a big boat or a little boat?" "Where did they go on the boat?"

Puppetelling: Tell the rhyme while using the Duck Stick Puppet and Box Boat. Undulate the ship up and down over the waves of a pretend ocean. The children can all play the White Mice, without puppets, while standing behind the Ship. Pop out the Duck at the end of the rhyme. (A basket of apples would add a nice touch to this rhyme to give to the Mice afterwards.)

Puppetmaking: Have the children make their own ships from shoe boxes. Then ask them to each think up and create an accompanying Captain Stick Puppet, other than a Duck. For example, a dog, a frog, or elephant.

Materials — Construction paper; and drinking straw or blunt skewer for rod control.

Construction — Cut out and color a Captain character image; attach to end of a rod control.

To Make Ship — Cut out and color ship's sails. Attach a stick on to the upper back of a shoe box or other type of box. Cut out a small hole in bottom of box to insert Stick Puppet through and pop puppet up and down.

To Make Duck Captain — Cut out and color a photocopy of Duck pattern. Attach to a rod control.

Puppetizing: Pretend that the classroom is a big sea. Let the children take turns playing the lead using their Captain puppets as the rhyme is recited. The rest of the group can play the mice without puppets. Be sure to change the words in the rhyme to match each new Captain.

DUCK CAPTAIN PATTERN

Box Ship

34

THE HOUSE THAT JACK BUILT

This is the house that Jack built.
This is the malt,
That lay in the house that Jack built.

This is the rat,
That ate the malt,
That lay in the house that Jack built.

This is the cat,
That killed the rat,
That ate the malt,
That lay in the house that Jack built.

This is the dog,
That worried the cat,
That killed the rat,
That ate the malt,
That lay in the house that Jack built.

This is the cow with the crumpled horn,
That tossed the dog,
That worried the cat,
That killed the rat,
That ate the malt,
That lay in the house that Jack built.

This is the maiden all forlorn,
That milked the cow with the crumpled horn,
That tossed the dog,
That worried the cat,
That killed the rat,
That ate the malt,
That lay in the house that Jack built.

This is the man all tattered and torn,
That kissed the maiden all forlorn,
That milked the cow with the crumpled horn,
That tossed the dog,
That worried the cat,
That killed the rat,
That ate the malt,
That lay in the house that Jack built.

This is the priest all shaven and shorn,
That married the man all tattered and torn,
That kissed the maiden all forlorn,
That milked the cow with the crumpled horn,
That tossed the dog,
That worried the cat,
That killed the rat,

That ate the malt,
That lay in the house that Jack built.

This is the cock that crowed in the morn,
That waked the priest all shaven and shorn,
That married the man all tattered and torn,
That kissed the maiden all forlorn,
That milked the cow with the crumpled horn,
That tossed the dog,
That worried the cat,
That killed the rat,
That ate the malt,
That lay in the house that Jack built.

This is the farmer sowing the corn,
That kept the cock that crowed in the morn,
That waked the priest all shaven and shorn,
That married the man all tattered and torn,
That kissed the maiden all forlorn,
That milked the cow with the crumpled horn,
That tossed the dog,
That worried the cat,
That killed the rat,
That ate the malt,
That lay in the house that Jack built.

Introducing the Rhyme: Tell the children that you have a funny poem to share with them. Explain some of the following terms: *Malt, Crumpled horn, Shaven and shorn, Cock that crowed,* and *Sowing the corn.*

Puppetelling: Recite the poem using a box house as a central prop and Cup Puppets of the characters on the tabletop. Put the malt inside the house. Hide the characters beforehand and take them out, one by one, as they appear in the rhyme, maneuvering them along the tabletop and into Jack's house.

Puppetmaking: Let each child make a Paper Cup Puppet of a favorite character from the rhyme.

Materials — Paper cup; and construction paper.

Construction — Color and cut out a character image. Add paper features and attach character to the paper cup. Glide the Cup Puppet along the table surface.

To Make Jack's House: — Use a cardboard house and cut out a peak for front of house from paper or poster board; attach to upper front of box. Cut out a door hole, partially, so that it will open and close and hinge on the fold edge as shown. Decorate the house with paper windows, shingles, bricks, etc.

Puppetizing: Call the children back to the playing circle. Ask several of the children to form a house shape with their bodies. Put the malt inside the house. Let the remaining children play the characters holding the Cup Puppets over the top of their hands. Each child can mimic the sounds or actions of the character as it goes into Jack's house.

Jack's House

Cardboard

malt

paper

yarn

Cup Puppets

36

HUMPTY DUMPTY

Humpty Dumpty sat on a wall,
Humpty Dumpty had a great fall;
All the King's horses, and all the King's men,
Cannot put Humpty Dumpty together again.

Introducing the Rhyme: Ask the children, "What is Humpty Dumpty?" "What happens to an egg if it falls on the ground?" "Can it be put back together again?"

Puppetelling: Make a wall out of cardboard or a small box, of if you have an apron, a felt wall can be attached to the bib. While reciting the poem, set your Humpty Dumpty Finger Puppet on top of the wall. Drop him onto your lap with his great fall. Then open him up to reveal the surprise yolk inside!

Puppetmaking: Let the children make Humpty Dumpty Stick Puppets to fall off the wall.

Materials — White construction paper; and drinking straw, blunt skewer, or stick for rod control.

Construction — Cut out a large egg shape from white paper. Color an egg yolk on one side of paper and a Humpty Dumpty character on the other; add features and a funny hat, bow tie or other costume. Attach to a rod control.

To Make Humpty Dumpty Finger Puppet — Cut out and color a photocopy of the Humpty Dumpty pattern. Color face and costume on one side and an egg yolk on the other. (Crayons are recommended as a coloring medium for this pattern so that colors will not soak through paper.) Fold down the two end sections of egg to hide yolk inside. Cut out finger holes and insert fingers through holes for legs.

Puppetizing: Invite the children back to the playing circle. Select a puppeteer to play Humpty Dumpty with the Stick Puppet. Have two children represent a wall with their arms and bodies. Let them act out the rhyme, beginning with the Humpty Dumpty side facing out and ending with the yolk side showing, while the other children recite it. Extend the activity by improvising the scene with additional children playing the King's men and horses trying to put Humpty together again.

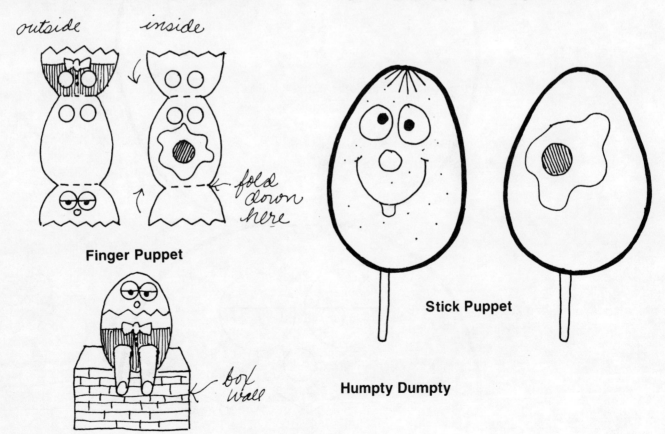

Finger Puppet

Stick Puppet

Humpty Dumpty

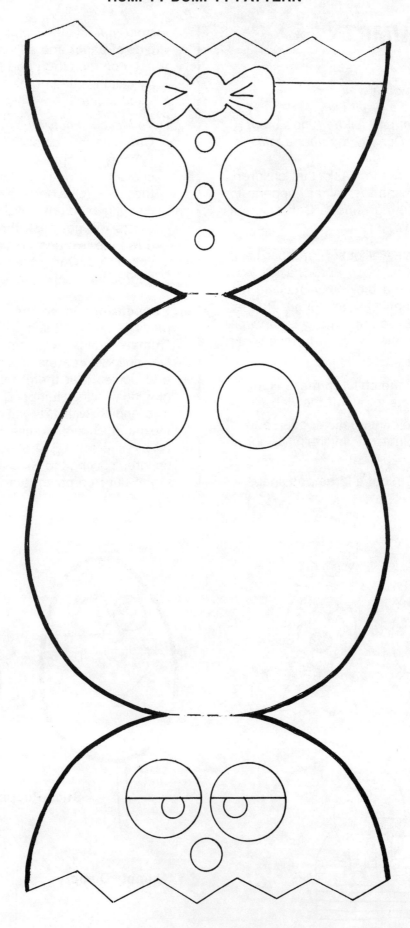

JACK AND JILL

Jack and Jill went up the hill,
To fetch a pail of water;
Jack fell down and broke his crown,
And Jill came tumbling after.

Then up Jack got, and home did trot,
As fast as he could caper,
They put him to bed and patched his head,
With vinegar and brown paper.

Introducing the Rhyme: Ask the children, "Have you ever fallen down and hurt your head?" "What did your mom or dad do to help you feel better?" "Did you ever have a bandage put on your head?" Discuss the word "crown" and how a long time ago, when they didn't have bandages, they used a piece of paper soaked in vinegar when someone was hurt.

Puppetelling: Invite one child to form a hill with his body and another child to pretend to be the bed. Using Jack and Jill Mitt Puppets, recite the poem while the puppets mime the actions up and down the child-hill and finally into the bed.

The leader can be the doctor who fixes Jack's head at the end of the rhyme. Put a strip of paper with a piece of double-stick masking tape attached to it onto Jack's head.

Puppetmaking: Ask each child to make a Jack or Jill Mitt Puppet to use for going up and down the hill.

Materials — Two photocopies of Mitt pattern; yarn; and coloring medium.

Construction — Put the two pattern pieces together and staple or glue around the outer edges, leaving bottom and arm holes open. Color in a face and costume; add yarn hair. To operate, insert three fingers up neck and use thumb and pinky for puppet's arms.

Puppetizing: Select puppeteers to play Jack and Jill with their Mitt Puppets. Ask another child to become the Doctor without a puppet. Two other children can represent the hill and bed with their bodies. Let the children take turns being the puppeteers and act out the rhyme. Encourage dialogue at the end of the rhyme between Jack, Jill, and the Doctor characters.

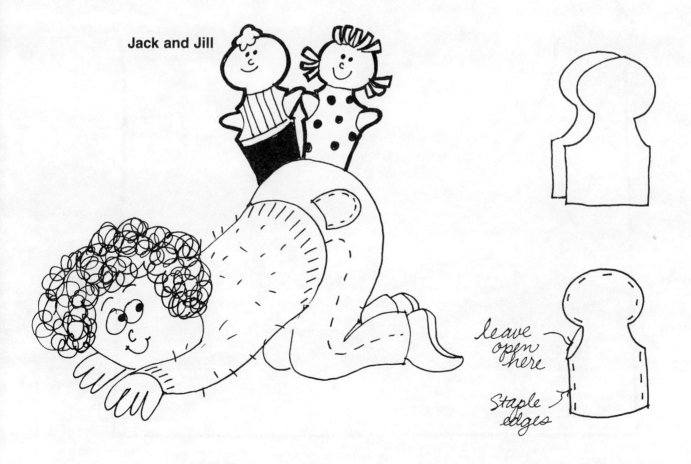

Jack and Jill

leave open here

staple edges

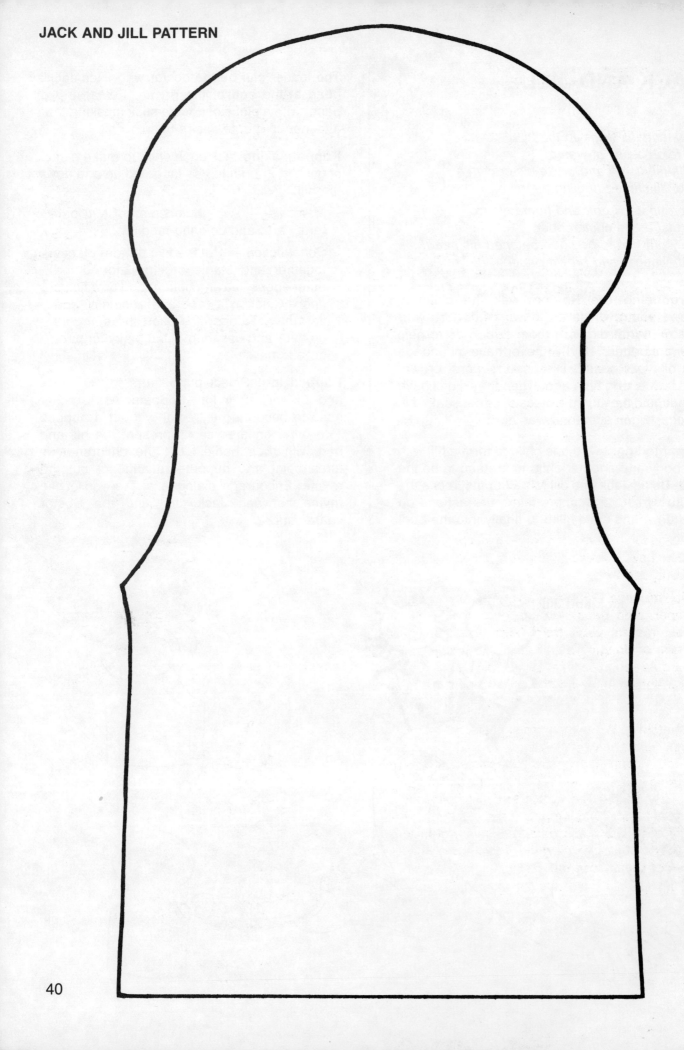

JACK BE NIMBLE

Jack be nimble,
Jack be quick,
Jack jump over
The candlestick.

Introducing the Rhyme: Ask the children, "What is the *biggest* thing you have ever jumped over?" Let the children show you how high they can jump (one at a time if space is limited). Explain the word "nimble."

Puppetelling: Using a Jack Box Puppet and a real or cardboard tube candlestick, say the rhyme as you mime the actions over your lapboard or tabletop. Then let the children suggest other ways that Jack could get to the other side of the candlestick, for example, by going *under, around, to the left* or *to the right of* your candlestick. Recite the poem again incorporating the children's suggestions.

Puppetmaking: Let each child make their own Jack Box Puppet with which to pantomime the actions.

   Materials — Cereal, cake, pudding or other food box; construction paper; and scrap fabric and trims.

   Construction — Paint or cover the box with paper. Add paper features and create a costume for Jack from fabric and trim. Yarn or fringed paper makes excellent hair. Attach paper feet to the bottom of the box and maneuver Jack around on a flat surface.

Jack Box Puppet

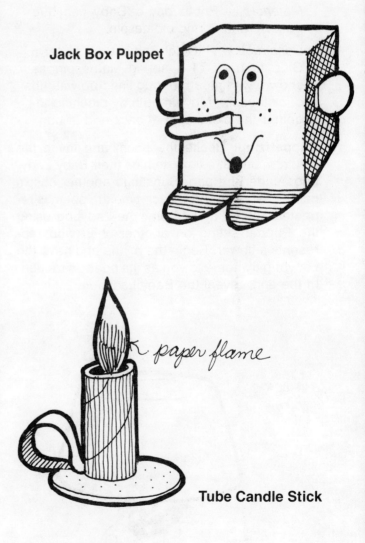

a paper flame

Tube Candle Stick

Puppetizing: While they are seated around the playing circle, ask the children to look around the room and find something that their Jack Puppet can jump over, such as as book, toy, or chair. Let each child take a turn showing how his Jack puppet can jump over the selected object. Recite the poem, changing the words to match the object. Don't worry if each new word does not rhyme with the verse.

LADYBUG, LADYBUG

Ladybug, ladybug, fly away home!
Your house is on fire, your children all gone,
All but one, and her name is Ann,
And she crept under the pudding pan.

Introducing the Rhyme: Talk about "hiding" with the children and ask, "What is your favorite hiding place?" "Where do you suppose little bugs like to hide?"

Puppetelling: Show the children your "pudding pan" (real pan or your cupped hand) with the Baby Ladybug Clothespin Puppet hidden underneath.

Puppetmaking: Have the children make their own Baby Ladybug Clothespin Puppets to hide under the pudding pan.

Materials — Photocopy of Baby Ladybug pattern; and spring clothespin.

Construction — Color and cut out pattern. Glue to back of a spring clothespin as shown, with mouth of bug lined up with tip of clothespin. Move mouth by pinching together the clothespin at back end of bug.

Puppetizing: Recite the poem and invite the children, one at a time, to hide their Baby Ladybugs under the pan. Substitute another child's name (instead of Ann) each time the poem is repeated. Or, let a child play the Ladybug using the Puppet sitting on another child who represents a flower. Begin the rhyme and have the Ladybug fly home to you as the poem is recited. In the end, reveal the Baby Ladybug.

Ladybug

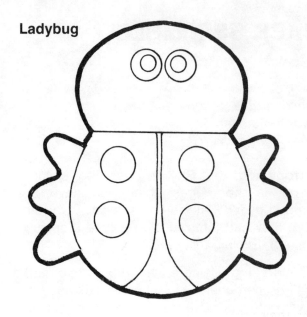

Baby Ladybug

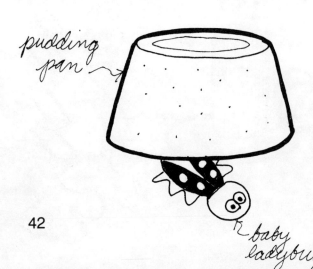

pudding pan

baby ladybug

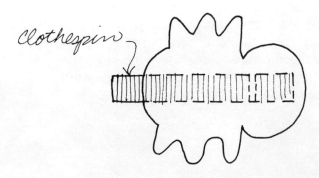

clothespin

THE LITTLE BIRD

Once I saw a little bird
Come hop, hop, hop;
So I cried, "Little bird,
Will you stop, stop, stop?"

I was going to the window
To say, "How do you do?"
But he shook his little tail,
And far away he flew.

Introducing the Rhyme: Ask the children to close their eyes and imagine the most wonderful bird in the world. "What color is it?" "How does it move?" Have the children demonstrate with their bodies how a bird hops around on the ground. Hide the Bird puppet in your pocket.

Puppetelling: Surprise the children by bringing out your Little Bird Envelope Puppet. Follow the rhyme's actions with the puppet ending it by tucking the "Little Bird" back into your pocket.

Puppetmaking: Ask the children to make their own Little Bird Envelope Puppets to hop in the rhyme.

Materials — 6½ x 3½ inch envelope; and construction paper.

Construction — Tuck flap inside envelope as shown. Place hand inside envelope and gently "bite" finger of other hand to form mouth; straighten out mouth if wrinkled. Color in features and beak. Add overly long, bouncy, pleated paper strip legs, and paper wings.

Puppetizing: When the children are seated around the playing circle, divide them into groups of three. Within each group, one child plays the puppeteer using the Bird puppet, another forms a window with the arms, and a third approaches the Bird from the opposite side of the window to say "How do you do?"

Follow-up dialogue can be encouraged by asking the children their puppets' names and questions like:

"Where are you flying today?"
"What did you eat for breakfast?"
"Where is your nest?" (a place in the room)
"Who lives in your nest with you?"

Then have each child hop to her nest and back again.

Little Bird Envelope Puppet

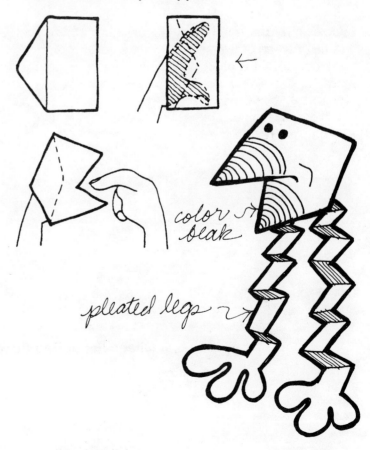

color beak

pleated legs

LITTLE BO-PEEP

I'm Little Bo-Peep, I've lost my sheep,
And can't tell where to find them;
If I leave them alone,
They'll come home,
And bring their tails behind them.

Introducing the Rhyme: Ask the children, "Have you ever lost someone like your mom or dad or even a pet before?" "How did you feel when you discovered you lost them?" "When you found them?"

Puppetelling: Change the verse to the first person so that you can portray Little Bo Peep telling the rhyme. Use two Sheep Paper-Bag Puppets and give the tails to two children to hold. Put both Sheep puppets on your hands and hide them either behind your back or in the puppet apron. Recite the poem and surprise the children at the end by bringing out the Sheep puppets. Ask the two assigned children to re-attach the tails where they belong.

Puppetmaking: Have the children make Sheep Paper-Bag Puppets for using in the rhyme.

Materials — Paper bags (preferably white); cotton or poly fiber; construction paper; and masking tape.

Construction — Glue bits of cotton or poly fiber to bags for sheep wool. (If materials are scarce, one or two cotton ball puffs for each child will suffice). Add paper ears and color in features. Make tail from white paper and add a piece of masking tape to end for attaching to sheep later. Put finger inside bag's flap and move up and down to operate.

Puppetizing: Invite the children back to the playing circle and ask them to hide the the puppets behind their backs. Recite the poem again, expressing delight at the end when you see all your returned sheep as the children pop them out. Encourage dialogue by asking them individually, "Where did you go?" "What did you do?" "Were you afraid?" "Were you really lost?"

Expand the activity by letting the children hide with their Sheep puppets somewhere in the room as if actually lost. They will enjoy your frantic calling and searching for them. Once they come home, attach their tails to them.

cotton

paper ears

Sheep Paper-Bag Puppet

44

LITTLE BOY BLUE

Little Boy Blue,
Come blow your horn!
The cow's in the meadow,
The sheep's in the corn.
But where is the little boy,
Tending the sheep?
Under the haystack,
Fast asleep!
Will you wake him?
No, not I,
For if I do,
He's sure to cry.

Introducing the Rhyme: Ask the children, "What are some of your favorite places for being alone or hiding?" Discuss haystacks with the children and what they are used for. "Have you ever been in a haystack?"

Puppetelling: Show the children your box haystack and recite the rhyme and surprise everyone at the end by revealing Little Boy Blue Paper Puppet hidden underneath.

Puppetmaking: Ask each child to make a Little Boy or Girl puppet, choosing a specific color for the costume such as blue, red, or orange.

Materials — Photocopies of asleep/awake Little Child patterns; and coloring medium.

Construction — Cut out and color the Little Child patterns. Glue patterns back to back to make a turn-around puppet. Cut out nose hole for inserting finger.

Puppetizing: Invite the children back to the playing circle with their Little Child puppets. Hide the puppets, one at a time, under the haystack and repeat the rhyme for each puppet, substituting its gender and color. For example, Little Boy Green, Little Girl Red, Little Boy Yellow, etc. Each puppet can be turned around at the end to show it is awake. The children will also enjoy showing how their puppets' noses wiggle.

LITTLE BOY BLUE PATTERNS

finger nose
crease here

cut nose hole

45

LITTLE JACK HORNER

Little Jack Horner,
Sat in the corner,
Eating of Christmas pie;
He put in his thumb,
And pulled out a plum,
And said, "What a good boy am I!"

Introducing the Rhyme: Ask the children, "What is your favorite kind of pie?" "How many of you have ever helped make a pie?" "What kinds of things can be put into a pie?" Talk about plums and explain to them what a plum looks and tastes like. Possibly bring in some real plums for the children to taste.

Puppetelling: Hide the paper plum in a pie tin and cover with a circular yellow felt or paper crust. Attach the Jack Finger Puppet to your first finger. Show the children your plum pie. Introduce Jack to them and recite the poem as you pull out the paper plum and hold it up for the children to see. Don't forget to use a contrasting voice when Jack says, "What a good boy am I!"

Puppetmaking: Each child can make a Jack or "Self" Finger Puppet and paper plum to use with the rhyme.

Materials — Actual photo of child or photocopy of Jack pattern; paper plum; and sticky-backed masking tape.

Construction — Cut out head of the child's photograph or cut out and color Jack's pattern. With sticky-backed tape attach face to first finger.

To Make Plums — Cut out circular paper plums. Put a piece of double-stick masking tape on the back of each one.

Puppetizing: Hide all the plums in the pan under the crust. Gather the children around the playing circle with their Jack or "Self" Puppets on their fingers. First pretend that you are baking the pie (in a make-believe box oven). Take the pie out and, one by one, invite the children up to act out the poem while everyone recites it. Be sure to substitute the child's name for 'Jack' and have each child put a thumb into the pan for a plum.

LITTLE JACK HORNER PATTERN

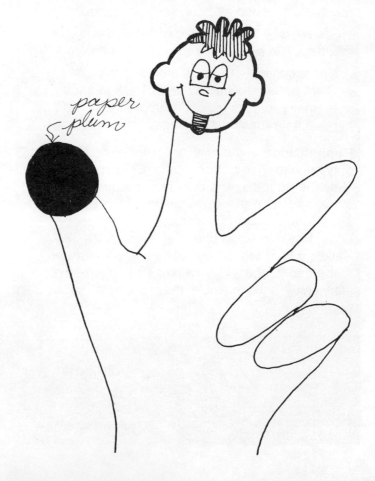

paper plum

LITTLE MISS MUFFET

Little Miss Muffet sat on a tuffet,
Eating her curds and whey;
There came a big spider,
Who sat down beside her,
And frightened Miss Muffet away.

Introducing the Rhyme: Discuss with the children, the interesting things spiders do and how they spin their beautiful webs. "Have you ever seen a web?" "Where?" "Why do you suppose we are sometimes afraid of spiders?" "Can you think of some good things that spiders do for people?" Show the children your Spider Finger Puppet and together count the eight legs.

Puppetelling: Establish from the beginning that the Spider is shy and wants to find a friend. Assign a child to be the puppeteer and operate Spider Finger Puppet while you play Miss Muffet, using a mixing bowl and spoon for props. When the Spider comes close to you, screech and run away. The children will enjoy watching you pretend to be frightened. The children may also want to play Little Miss Muffet while *you* be the Spider.

Puppetmaking: Let each child make a Big Spider Bodi-Bag Spider from a supermarket bag to scare away Miss Muffet.

Materials — Large supermarket bag; construction paper; 2½ foot long fabric strip or ribbons for necktie; and eight 1 inch wide paper strips for legs.

Construction — Decorate the bags with paint or other coloring mediums by splashing or coloring textures and colors over the Spider's body. Add facial features to upper flap of bag and attach pleated paper strip legs to the sides of bag. Staple center of necktie to center top of bag and attach to child's neck.

To Make Spider Finger Puppet — Cut out and color the Spider pattern. Make a finger tube by rolling up a 1 inch strip of paper and attaching to back of Spider. Add eight yarn legs.

Puppetizing: Back at the playing circle, have each child think up a name for his Big Spider puppet and introduce it. Act out the verse repeatedly so each child has a turn to incorporate the Spider's name into the rhyme. For example: *"Along came a Big Spider, named Jo-Jo, etc."* Encourage dialogue at the end by asking why the Spider came to visit. Resolve each interaction by becoming friends to help establish more positive feelings towards spiders.

yarn legs

paper finger tube

SPIDER PATTERN

neck tie

pleated legs

Spider Bodi-Bag Puppet

THE LITTLE MOUSE

I have seen you, little mouse,
Running all about the house;
Through the hole your little eye,
In the wainscot peeping sly,
Hoping soon some crumbs to steal,
To make quite a hearty meal.
Look before you venture out,
See if pussy is about.
If she's gone, you'll quickly run,
To the larder for some fun;
Round about the dishes creep,
Taking into each a peep,
To choose the daintiest that's there,
Spoiling things you do not care.

Introducing the Rhyme: Ask the children, "Have you ever seen a mouse?" "Where do you think mice like to hide?" "What do they like to eat?"

Puppetelling: Recite the rhyme with the Little Mouse Finger Puppet while randomly peeking it through the living room scene of the Peek-a-Boo Board at appropriate times. Turn the board around to reveal the kitchen scene on the other side for the last half of the poem.

Puppetmaking: Have each child make a Little Mouse Envelope Puppet to run through the house. (See page 60).

Materials — 6½ x 3½ inch envelope; construction paper; and yarn.

Construction — Seal envelope and fold in half, crosswise; crease fold. Slit creased line on outside only. Add paper mouse ears, yarn whiskers and other features. Put the fingers in upper section of envelope and thumb in lower, to operate mouth.

To Make Little Mouse Finger Puppet — Using pattern cut out a front and a back piece for mouse. Topstitch around outer edges, leaving bottom open for finger. Add a button nose, yarn whiskers, plastic wiggle eyes and felt ears.

To Make Peek-a-Boo Board — Cut out and color photocopies of the kitchen and living room scenes. Use rubber cement and glue one scene to the back of a sheet of poster board or other lightweight cardboard. Cut out peek holes (heavy lined areas). Line up and glue the second scene to the other side of cardboard. Cut out peek holes for that side.

Puppetizing: Hide a number of pieces of cheese and bread at random around the room. Then have the children, with their Mice puppets, search for these delectable tidbits while you recite the poem.

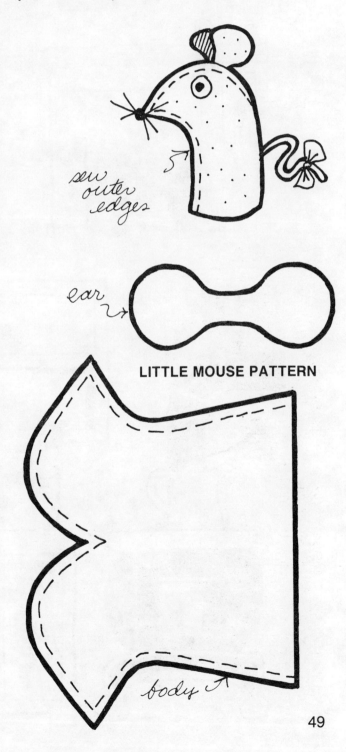

sew outer edges

ear

LITTLE MOUSE PATTERN

body

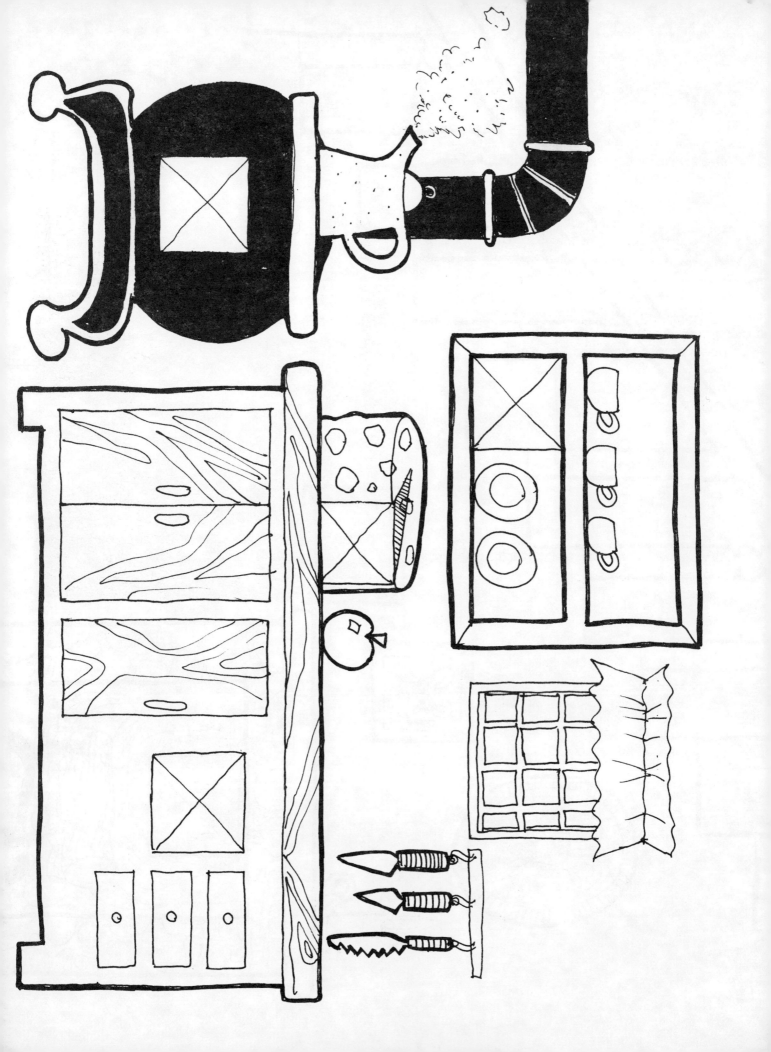

THE MAN IN THE MOON

The Man in the Moon looked out of the moon,
Looked out of the moon and said,
" 'Tis time for all children on the earth,
To think about getting to bed!"

Introducing the Rhyme: Ask the children what they like best about the moon? What do they think of when they look up at the moon at night? Do they sometimes see a face on the moon?

Puppetelling: Hide your Man Stick Puppet behind the Paper-Plate Moon and recite the poem as you peek your puppet out.

Puppetmaking: Have the children make up a Stick Puppet of another person or creature that could live on the Moon.

Materials — Paper plate; and blunt skewer or cardboard towel tube for rod control.

Construction — Make a face by adding features to a paper plate with paper or coloring medium; attach to the end of a rod control.

To Make Moon — Color a paper plate yellow and add simple facial features; attach to a rod cntrol.

Puppetizing: Call the children back to the playing circle and repeat the rhyme, substituting each new character while changing the words to match. The child whose turn it is can hide her puppet behind the Moon puppet and act out the rhyme as it is recited.

Moon

paper plate

Stick Puppets

The Man in the Moon

53

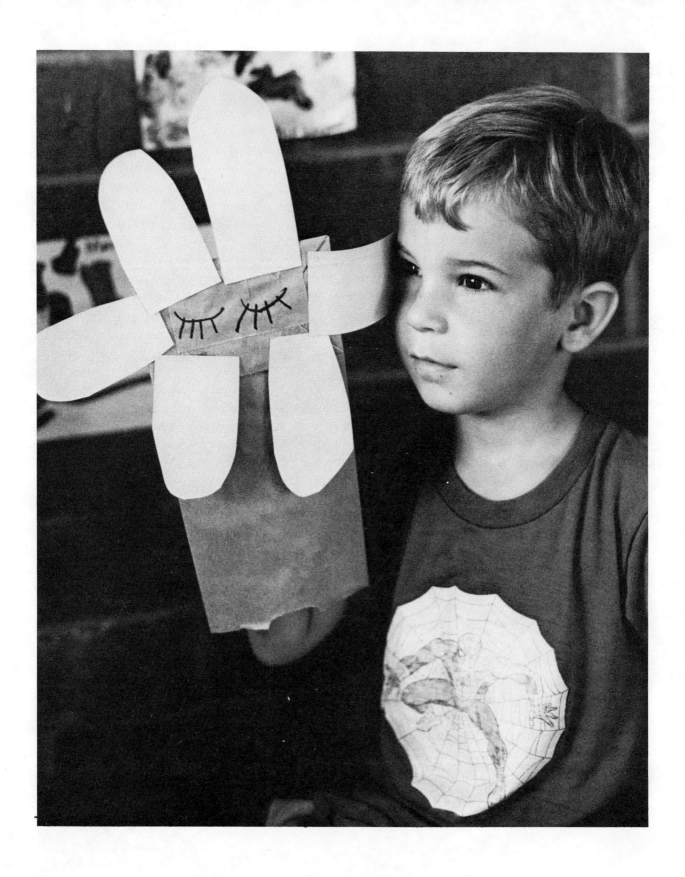

MARY, MARY, QUITE CONTRARY

Mary, Mary, quite contrary,
How does your garden grow?
Silver bells and cockle-shells,
And pretty maids all of a row.

Introducing the Rhyme: Ask the children to close their eyes and imagine that they are all sitting in a lovely garden. In that garden is a most beautiful flower. "What color is the flower?" "How does it smell?" "What do you need to plant to grow a flower?" "What do flowers need to help them grow?"

Puppetelling: Put your hand in a closed position and recite the rhyme to the children as you lift up each finger to reveal each Flower Finger Puppet.

Puppetmaking: Have the children create beautiful Flower Paper-Bag Puppets to grow in the garden.

Materials — Construction paper; and medium-sized paper bag.

Construction — Cut out colorful flower petals from paper. Glue petals around edges of upper flap of bag and lower section of bag just below the flap. Add a happy face. Put fingers inside bag and move up and down to operate flap-mouth.

To Make Flower Finger Puppets — Cut out and color a photocopy of each of the Flowers. Laminate in clear contact paper or plastic, if permanency is desired. Attach to a rubber household or other glove with double-stick tape.

Puppetizing: Invite the children back into the garden, lining them up in two rows. They should pretend to be seeds and curl their bodies up on the floor with their Flower puppets hidden beneath. The leader should pretend to plant the seeds one-by-one and water them with a watering can prop followed by waving a sun on a stick over them. Then recite the poem while the beautiful Flowers grow upwards and blossom very slowly.

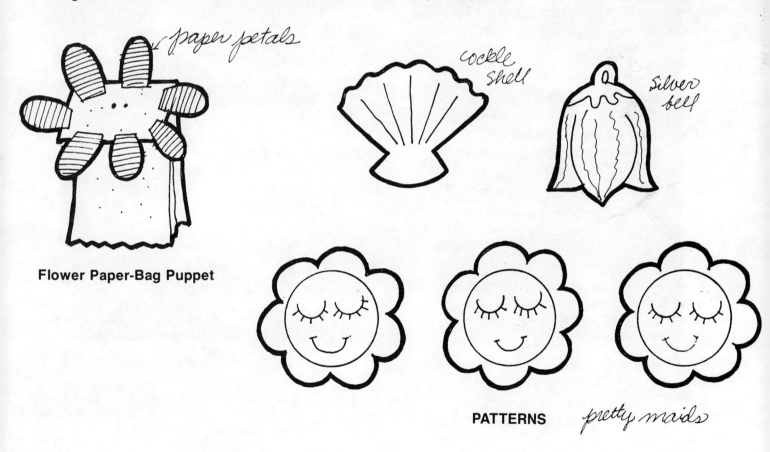

paper petals

Flower Paper-Bag Puppet

cockle shell

silver bell

PATTERNS *pretty maids*

55

THE MULBERRY BUSH

Here we go round the mulberry bush,
The mulberry bush, the mulberry bush;
Here we go round the mulberry bush,
On a cold and frosty morning.
(Brrr . . . Brrr . . . Brrr . . .)

This is the way we wash our hands,
Wash our hands, wash our hands;
This is the way we wash our hands,
On a cold and frosty morning.
(Brrr . . . Brrr . . . Brrr . . .)

This is the way we wash our clothes,
Wash our clothes, wash our clothes;
This is the way we wash our clothes,
On a cold and frosty morning.
(Brrr . . . Brrr . . . Brrr . . .)

This the way we go to school,
Go to school, go to school;
This is the way we go to school,
On a cold and frosty morning.
(Brrr . . . Brrr . . . Brrr . . .)

This is the way we come out of school,
Come out of school, come out of school;
This is the way we come out of school,
On a cold and frosty morning.
(Brrr . . . Brrr . . . Brrr . . .)

Introducing the Rhyme: Explain to the children what a mulberry bush is. Ask, "Do you have a favorite bush or tree that would be fun to dance around?" Then have them mime the following actions from the rhyme:

- *Wash our hands*
- *Wash our clothes*
- *Go to school*
- *Come out of school (on a cold, frosty morning)*

Puppetelling: Using any hand puppet and some doll clothes in a small basin as props, pantomime the actions over a lapboard while reciting the rhyme.

Puppetmaking: Have the children create Bodi-Bag Puppets of any character they choose for dancing around the Mulberry Bush.

Materials — Supermarket bag; construction paper; two 3 inch wide fabric strips (length of child's arm); two medium rubber bands; a 2½ foot fabric strip or ribbon for neck; and scrap fabrics and trims.

Construction — For arms, fold over the end of each fabric strip and slip a rubber band in each hem; staple hems to secure rubber bands. Staple other end of each arm strip to paper bag, just below the bag's flap. Attach the center neck ribbon to center top of bag. Decorate bag with coloring medium and scrap materials; add paper features. To wear, tie neck ribbon around the child's neck and slip rubber bands over wrists. The child can then pantomime the actions using his own legs.

Puppetizing: Call the children back to the playing circle. Ask one child to play the Mulberry Bush (either without a puppet or make a Bodi-Bag Bush puppet) and stand in the center. The rest of the children can pantomime the actions around the Bush while wearing their puppets.

This activity could be repeated with a thematic selection of the characters such as monsters, zoo animals, or farmers. Also holiday characters such as Witches and Reindeer make excellent groupings. Let the children think up something other than a Mulberry Bush for the character to go around. Such as a:

- *Barn for the farmers.*
- *Christmas Tree for the Reindeer.*
- *Cauldron of Witch's brew for the Witches.*

Also consider changing some of the words in the rhyme to suit the actions of the characters. Such as:

- *This is the way we hoe our crops (farmers)*
- *This is the way we pull our sled (Reindeer)*
- *This is the way we stir our brew (Witches)*

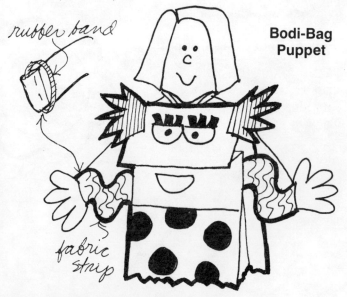

rubber band

fabric strip

Bodi-Bag Puppet

OLD KING COLE

Old King Cole was a merry old soul,
And a merry old soul was he;
He called for his pipe,
And he called for his bowl,
And he called for his fiddlers three.

And every fiddler, he had a fine fiddle,
And a very fine fiddle had he;
"Twee tweedle dee, tweedle dee,"
  went the fiddlers.
Oh, there's none so rare as can compare,
With King Cole and his fiddlers three.

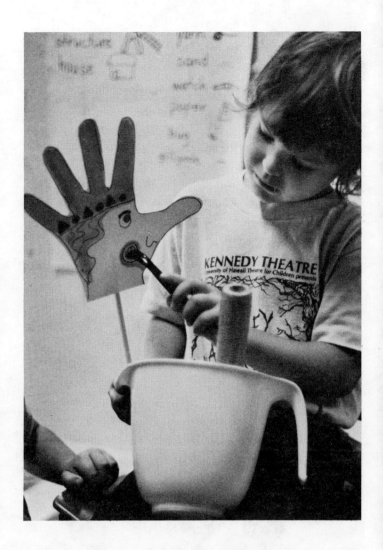

Introducing the Rhyme: Ask the children, "If you were a King and could have anything you wanted, what would you wish for?" Talk about a "fiddle" and be sure the children know what it is. Let them all pretend to play a fiddle together.

Puppetelling: Give two children the bowl and pipe props to hold. Bring out your Old King Cole Hand Puppet and recite the poem while two assigned children carry up the two props. Ask three children to play the fiddles, without puppets.

Puppetmaking: Have the children create their own Old King Cole or Queen Cole Hand Puppets to act out the parts.

Old King Cole Hand Puppet

> *Materials* — Construction paper; drinking straw or blunt skewer for rod control; and sequins (optional).

> *Construction* — Lay hand flat on paper and trace a line around the outside edges of hand and fingers. Cut out and decorate the face and crown areas (the fingers represent the crown and thumb the nose.) Attach to end of a rod control.

Puppetizing: Ask each child to play the King or Queen (change the words in verse to suit gender and character) while the poem is recited by the group. Each new King or Queen may be asked to call for something else desired from around the room. Another child could carry the item to the royal character, replacing the words "pipe" or "bowl" with the name of this new item (book, ring, toy car, etc.).

OLD MOTHER HUBBARD

I'm Old Mother Hubbard, I went to the cupboard,
To give my poor dog a bone;
But when I got there the cupboard was bare,
And so my poor dog had none.
(Boo-hoo, Boo-hoo, Boo-hoo.)

I went to the Baker to buy him some bread;
When I came back the poor dog was dead.
(Boo-hoo, Boo-hoo, Boo-hoo.)

I went to the Undertaker to buy him a coffin;
When I came back the dog was laughing.
(Ha, Ha, Ha — Ha, Ha, Ha.)

I went to the Hatter to buy him a hat;
When I came back he was feeding the cat.

I went to the Cobbler to buy him some shoes;
When I came back he was reading the news.
(Mumbling sounds.)

I went to the Tailor to buy him a coat;
But when I came back he was riding a goat.
(Rides goat.)

I went to the Grocer to buy him some fruit;
When I came back he was playing the flute.
(Play flute.)

I went to the Fishmonger to buy him some fish;
But when I came back he was licking the dish.
(Licks dish.)

I went to the Barber to buy him a wig;
When I came back he was dancing a jig.
(Play kazoo or noise maker.)

I made a curtsy, my dog made a bow;
I said, "Your servant,"
My dog said — "Bow-wow, bow-wow, wow,
    wow, wow, WOW!"

58

Introducing the Rhyme: Ask the children, "How many of you have a pet dog?" "What is your dog's name?" "Can your dog do tricks?" Ask the children to become dogs and one at a time enter the playing circle to make up and perform a trick for the group.

Puppetelling: You will need the following props: bonnet or wig and old lady glasses; real or imaginary cupboard; toy flute, kazoo, or other similar noise maker; small newspaper; dish; and a stuffed toy or hand puppet dog and cat.

Put on the bonnet or wig and glasses and take on the role of Old Mother Hubbard. Use the dog as you act out the different verses of the rhyme. Let the actions take place over your lapboard and integrate the props listed.

Puppetmaking: Have the children create the following Bodi-Bag characters from supermarket bags: Dog, Baker, Undertaker, Hatter, Cat, Cobbler, Tailor, Goat, Fruiterer, Fishmonger and Barber. If you wish to include the entire class, consider putting more than one shopkeeper in each shop or think up additional shopkeepers and verses to add to the original rhyme.

Materials — Large grocery bag; two medium rubber bands; two 3 inch wide fabric strips (length of child's arms); a 2½ foot long fabric strip or ribbon for necktie; and scrap paper, fabric and trims.

Construction — For arms: Fold over the end of each fabric strip and slip a rubber band in each hem; staple hems to secure rubber bands. Staple the other end of each arm strip to paper bag, just below the bag's flap. Attach the center neck ribbon to center top of bag. Add paper or fabric features and appropriate shopkeeper's costumes and hats. To wear, tie neck ribbon around the child's neck and slip rubber bands over wrists. The child then can pantomime the actions using her own legs.

Puppetizing: Take on the role of Mother Hubbard, this time letting a child play the Dog wearing a Bodi-Puppet. Assign the roles of the shopkeepers to other children also wearing Bodi-Puppets. Arrange each shopkeeper and "shop" around the playing space in order of appearance with suitable props, such as a loaf of bread for the baker, shoe-box coffin for the undertaker, and fruits for the fruiterer. Act out the rhyme while you visit each shopkeeper.

Encourage dialogue and interact with each character as you go along, especially the Dog.

rubber band

Old Mother Hubbard

Bodi-Bag Puppets

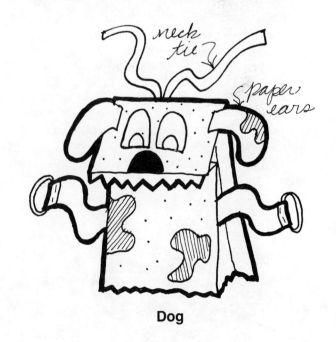

neck tie

paper ears

Dog

ONE TO TEN

1, 2, 3, 4, 5!
I caught a hare alive;
6, 7, 8, 9, 10!
I let her go again.

Introducing the Rhyme: Ask the children, "Can you think of some creatures that you would like to catch?" Show the children your net (or use a rice strainer with a handle) and ask them what some good things would be to catch in it.

Puppetelling: Recite the verse several times while putting out a variety of creatures (puppets, stuffed toys, or pictures, one by one) from your apron pockets or other hidden source. Catch each creature with the net and let it go again. Change the words in the poem to match each new character. For example: butterfly, bee, bug, hare, fish, and firefly.

Puppetmaking: Ask the children to make Envelope Puppets of a creature that they would like to catch with the net.

Materials — 6½ x 3½ inch envelope; and construction paper.

Construction — Seal envelope and fold in half crosswise with sealed flap side underneath; crease fold. Slit creased fold line on outside of envelope only. Add features, wings, tails, etc. with paper or coloring medium. To operate, slip fingers in upper section of envelope and thumb in lower section; open and close hand.

Puppetizing: Seat the children around the playing circle. Repeat the verse while going around the circle catching everyone's puppet, one at a time, in the net. Be sure to change the words of the rhyme to correspond with each new character.

Envelope Puppets

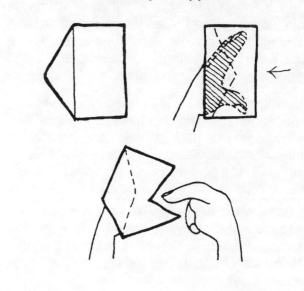

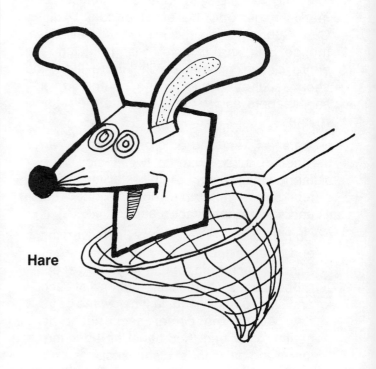

Hare

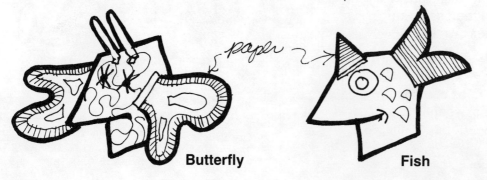

Butterfly

Fish

paper

Bee

PUSSYCAT, PUSSYCAT WHERE HAVE YOU BEEN?

Leader: *Pussycat, pussycat, where have you been?*

Pussycat: *I've been to London to visit the queen.* (Meow sweetly)

Leader: *Pussycat, pussycat, what did you do there?*

Pussycat: *I frightened a little mouse from under her chair.* (Growl loudly)

Introducing the Rhyme: Ask the children, "Does anybody have a pet cat?" "What is your cat's name?" "What games do you play with your cat?" "Does your cat ever chase birds or bugs?"

Puppetelling: Put on the paper crown and play the Queen's role as you sit on a small chair with the Little Mouse Finger Puppet hidden underneath. Introduce the Pussycat Paper-Plate Puppet to the children. Recite the first line of the poem, "Pussycat, Pussycat, Where have you been?" Then respond with the Pussycat using dialogue in a contrasting voice, adding purring and meowing sounds. At the end of the poem, have the Pussycat chase away the Little Mouse from under the chair.

Puppetmaking: Ask each child to make a Pussycat Paper-Plate Puppet for chasing the Mouse.

Materials — Paper plate; construction paper; and yarn.

Construction — Fold paper plate in half. Add paper ears, and large eyes, yarn whiskers, and other details. To operate, hold puppet as shown and open and close hand.

For Finger Puppet Mouse — Refer to Hickory Dickory Dock for Mouse construction.

To Make Crown — Cut out a crown from gold paper and decorate with sequins or tinfoil.

Puppetizing: Back at the playing circle, invite the children to take turns playing the Pussycat. You recite the questions in the rhyme while the children respond with the answers using their Pussycat puppets. End the poem each time by letting the Pussycat frighten your Little Mouse from under your chair. The Pussycat and Mouse could become friends before the poem is replayed again. Ask each child to think of some way this friendship can be shared or expressed, such as giving a hug, sharing a secret, or snack.

fold line

Pussy Cat Paper-Plate Puppet

SING A SONG OF SIXPENCE

Sing a song of sixpence,
A pocket full of rye;
Four-and-twenty blackbirds,
Baked in a pie!

When the pie was opened,
The birds began to sing;
Wasn't that a dainty dish,
To set before the king?

The king was in his counting-house,
Counting out his money;
The queen was in the parlor,
Eating bread and honey.

The maid was in the garden,
Hanging out the clothes;
When down came a blackbird,
And snapped off her nose!

Introducing the Rhyme: Ask the children, "What do you suppose a blackbird looks like?" If possible show them some pictures of blackbirds. Talk about Kings, Queens, and especially parlors so that the children will have an understanding of the words in the rhyme.

Puppetelling: Put on a paper nose with double-backed tape and tell the children you will play the part of the Maid in the rhyme. Then divide the children into two groups. Ask one group to be Kings and demonstrate how they can count money. Ask the other group side to be Queens and show how they can eat bread and honey. Place an empty aluminum pie tin on your lapboard or lap. With the Blackbird Finger Puppet on your finger, place your hand in the tin and cover it with a piece of round felt crust. At the appropriate time in the rhyme, open the pie and let the Blackbird fly out singing, "Wasn't that a dainty dish to set before the king?" The Kings and Queens should act out the middle verses without puppets. End the rhyme by letting the Blackbird actually "peck" off your paper nose.

Puppetmaking: Have the children make their own Blackbird Finger Puppets to put in the pie.

Materials — Photocopy of pattern; and small rubber band.

Construction — Cut out and color the Bird pattern. Staple rubber band across back of bird and slip the first finger under it. The Blackbird can be made to "peck" or "sing" by moving the first finger and thumb together as shown.

To Make Crowns — Cut out two crowns from gold construction paper and decorate with sequins or tinfoil.

Puppetizing: Invite the children back to the playing circle. Select four children to play the King, Queen, Maid, and the Blackbird who pecks off the Maid's nose. Put crowns on the King and Queen and the paper nose on the Maid. Pretend that the playing circle is a gigantic pie and ask all the children to hide inside the pie with their Blackbird puppets. Have the children practice making bird sounds and singing, "Isn't that a dainty dish to set before the King?"

Two chairs may be set up as thrones with a pile of coins and actual bread and honey props. A clothesline with a basket of clothes to hang and clothespins would be fun to include. Arrange the King, Queen, and Maid at various locations around the playing space. Recite the poem as the Blackbirds fly out of the playing circle pie, singing. At the end, an assigned Blackbird should peck off the Maid's nose.

BLACKBIRD PATTERN

THE TARTS

The Queen of Hearts she made some tarts,
All on a summer's day;
The Knave of Hearts he stole the tarts,
And took them clean away.
The King of Hearts called for the tarts,
And beat the Knave full sore;
The Knave of Hearts brought back the tarts,
And vowed, "I'll steal no more!"

Introducing the Rhyme: Help the children grasp the concept of Royalty and what kinds of functions are performed by Kings, Queens, and Knaves. Explain to them what a tart is and what the various things are that can be put into tarts. The children might enjoy making tarts as part of a cooking activity. Simple tarts can be made by baking various sliced fruits on top of ready made frozen biscuit dough. If an oven is not available then flat round cookies may be used as tart bases.

Puppetelling: Arrange the real tarts on a lap-board or tabletop and recite the rhyme, interchanging the paper masks of the King, Queen and Knave in front of your face as you play each character.

Puppetmaking: Ask each child to make a Tart puppet from small paper plates for the Knave to steal.

Materials — Two small paper plates; and construction paper.

Construction — Put the plates together and staple together around outer edges, leaving bottom edge open for hand to slip through. Color in or cut out various fruit shapes from paper, such as cherries or peaches, to glue on plate. Add a funny face, if desired.

To Make Royalty Masks — Cut out large heart shapes from red paper. Cut out eye holes and add features and a crown; attach to cardboard towel tube or blunt skewer for rod control.

Puppetizing: Ask the children to be seated around the playing circle. Select three children to play the Royalty characters using the paper masks. Choose the rest of the children to be the Tarts and hold up their Tart puppets while standing in a row in an area designated as the kitchen. While the Queen is busy in the kitchen pretending to make the Tarts (some kitchen props such as a mixing bowl and spoon would be fun to add), the King could be sitting on his throne (chair). Recite the rhyme again as the children follow the actions.

Queen   Knave   King   Tart

HEART PATTERN

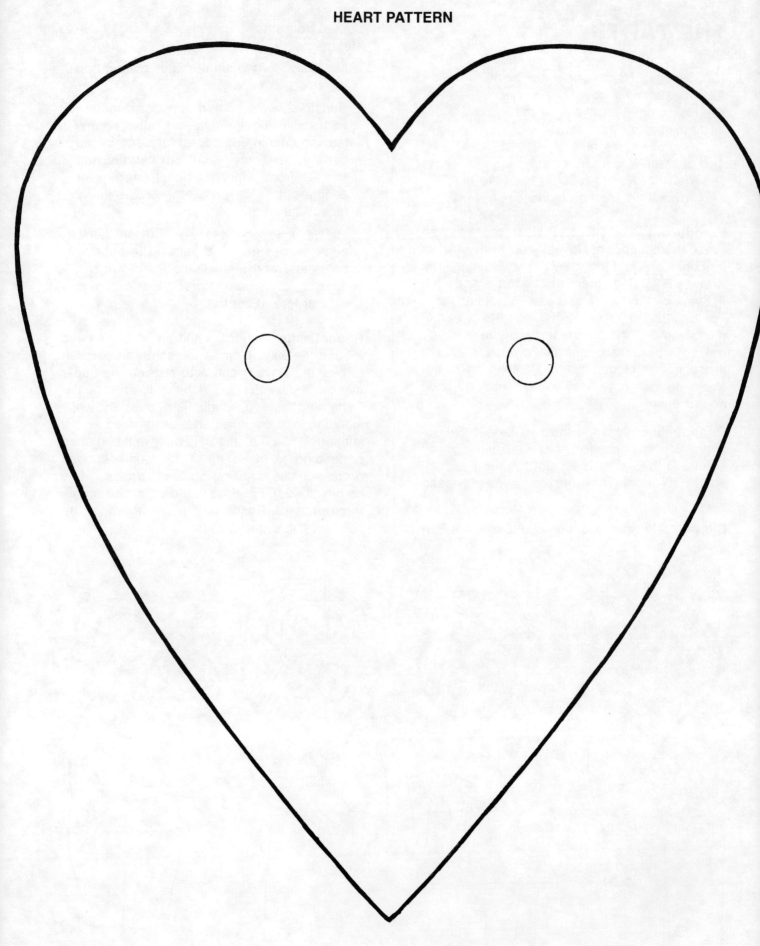

THERE WAS A CROOKED MAN

There was a crooked man,
And he went a crooked mile,
He found a crooked sixpence,
Against a crooked stile;
He bought a crooked cat,
Which caught a crooked mouse,
And they all lived together
In a little crooked house.

Introducing the Rhyme: Ask the children "Do you know what the word crooked means?" (There are two meanings of this word that can be discussed.) "Can you make different parts of your bodies crooked?" (For example—arms, legs, fingers.)

Puppetelling: Recite and dramatize the rhyme using the Crooked Man Paper Puppet, having two children play the parts of the Crooked Cat and Mouse without puppets, by forming their bodies into crooked shapes. Designate an area, such as a small rug, playhouse, or chair to represent the Crooked House. The Crooked Man can pretend to buy the Cat who in turn catches the Mouse and all live together in the house.

Puppetmaking: Have the children create Crooked String Puppets of characters that the Crooked Man could meet on his journey, such as a crooked cow, snake, or a giraffe.

Materials — Construction paper; string; and cardboard tube.

Construction — Cut out and color crooked shapes for characters from construction paper. A giraffe can have a crooked neck and a snake a crooked body. Attach one or two strings to top of shape and tie ends to a cardboard tube handle.

To Make Crooked Man Puppet — Cut out and color pattern pieces. Attach the top and bottom of the Crooked Man together at the waistline. Crease the fold lines on the man's mouth, as shown, and move fingers up and down behind mouth to operate.

Puppetizing: Retell the rhyme while adding new lines as the Crooked Man meets each new character. The line "He bought a crooked _____, which caught a crooked _____," may be repeated until all of the children have had a turn walking their puppets along the floor.

crooked snake

tube

crease lines

Crooked Man Puppet

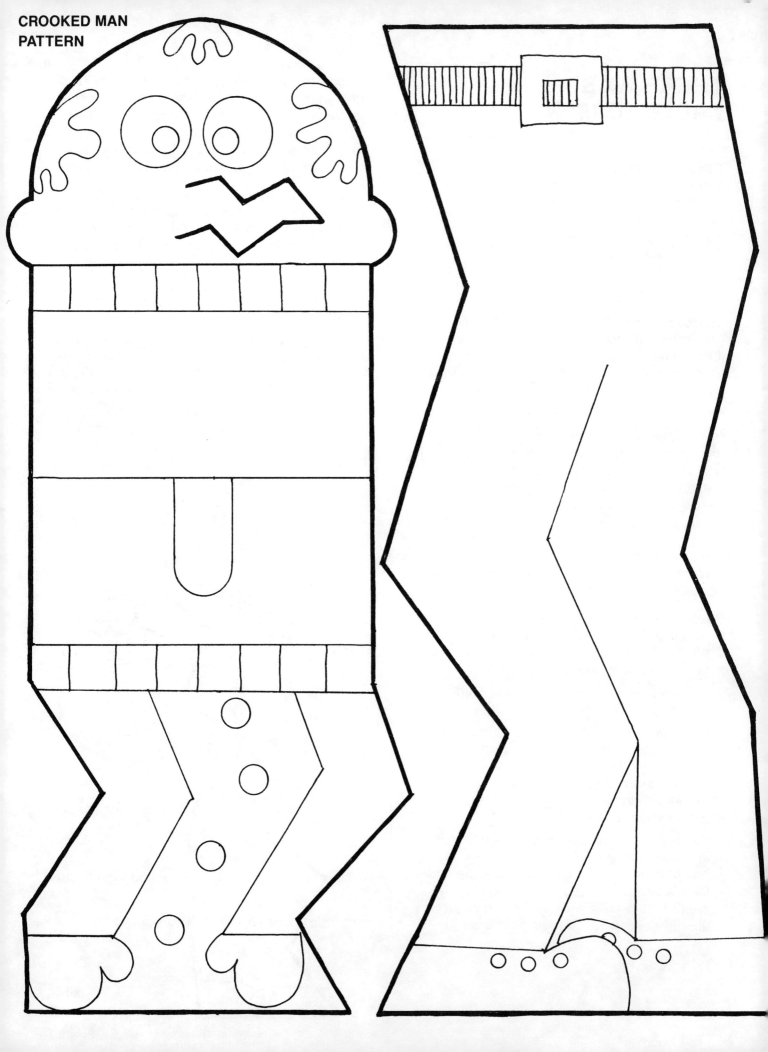

CROOKED MAN
PATTERN

THERE WAS
A LITTLE GIRL

There was a little girl,
Who had a little curl,
Right in the middle of her forehead.
When she was good,
She was very, very good,
But when she was bad she was horrid!

Introducing the Rhyme: Ask the children, "What does it mean when someone is a 'good' person?" "When someone is a 'horrid' person?" Talk about things the children do that make them feel "good" or "horrid" about themselves.

Puppetelling: Using a Turn-A-Round Paper-Plate Puppet, recite the rhyme with the "good" face showing and turn the puppet around to show the "horrid" face at the end.

Puppetmaking: Ask the children to make Turn-A-Round Puppets of themselves looking "good" on one side and "horrid" on the other.

Materials — Two paper plates; cardboard towel tube (optional); construction paper; and paper or wood shaving curls.

Construction — Put the two paper plates together and staple around the outer edges leaving the bottom edge open for inserting the hand, or glue a cardboard tube up inside, between the plates, as a rod control. Attach a curl to top of head. Create a "good" face on one side and a "horrid" face on the other.

Puppetizing: Call the children back to the playing circle and recite the rhyme with each child holding up the appropriate side of his or her puppet. (Change the gender of the poem to suit boys or girls). Upon completion of each recitation, have the child express one "good" deed the puppet can do with the group such as hug someone, share something, or say, "I like you."

staple around edges

tube

Little Girl Turn-A-Round Puppet

THERE WAS AN OLD WOMAN

I am an old woman who lives in a shoe,
I have so many children, and I know just
  what to do;
I give them some broth and a big slice
  of bread,
I kiss them all soundly and tuck them in bed.

Introducing the Rhyme: Have the children tell the number of children in each of their families. Ask them, "How many sisters or brothers do you have?" "What does your whole family like to do together?" "How do you sometimes help your brothers and sisters?"

Puppetelling: In this activity, have the group make the Children puppets beforehand. Recite the rhyme in the first person, thus taking on the role of the Old Woman, calling up each child with their puppet one at a time. Give the child's puppet a goodnight kiss and tuck it in bed inside your Shoe tote. Some pieces of bread may be put inside the shoe at the appropriate time.

Puppetmaking: Ask each child to make a Child Paper Finger Puppet to live in the shoe.

Materials — Construction paper; scrap fabric; and yarn.

Construction — Cut out and color a picture of a child character. Decorate with fabric and yarn. Roll up a 2 inch wide paper strip into a tube to fit finger; glue to back of character.

To Make Old Woman Puppet — Make photocopies of front and back of Old Woman patterns. Put pieces together and glue or staple around outer edges leaving bottom open for fingers.

To Make Shoe Tote — Use a real shoe or boot for a tote or decorate the outside of a medium-sized paper bag to look like a shoe with construction paper or coloring medium. Punch holes and tie on real shoelaces to give this tote a special touch!

Puppetizing: This is an activity without puppets. Ask the children to sit inside the playing circle and pretend they live inside a giant shoe. Take on the role of the Old Woman and recite the rhyme again. Go around to the children, giving them each a piece of bread, a goodnight kiss and tucking them into "bed." This would be a fun rhyme to use during snack or nap time. The words in the rhyme can be changed to match the snack food of the day. Children will also enjoy taking turns playing the Old Woman with a bonnet, glasses, and apron.

OLD WOMAN PATTERN

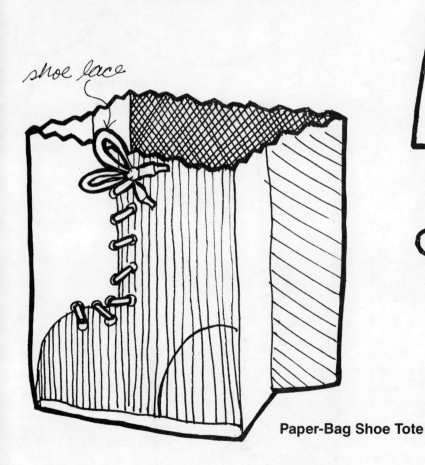

shoe lace

Paper-Bag Shoe Tote

THERE WAS ONCE A FISH

There was once a fish.
(What more could you wish?)
He lived in the sea.
(Where else would he be?)
He was caught on a line.
(Whose line if not mine?)
So I brought him to you.
(What else should I do?)

Introducing the Rhyme: Show the children your Sea Tote and ask them to think up all the things that live in the sea. "Have you ever caught a fish?" "How big was it?" "What color was it?" "Did you eat it or put it back in the water?"

Puppetelling: Hide the Fish inside an opened paper bag Sea Tote. Catch the Fish with your fishing rod while reciting the rhyme. Once caught, present the Fish to one of the children. You may wish to substitute the child's name at the end of the rhyme. The rhyme may be repeated with as many Fish as there are children.

Puppetmaking: Let each child make a Fish or other sealife Paper-Plate Puppet such as a jellyfish, crab, or clam. Encourage individual design in their colors and textures.

Materials — Two paper plates and construction paper.

Construction — Put the two plates together and staple around the outer edges, leaving one side open to slip the hand through. Add eyes, a paper tail, fins, and other features. Decorate gaily with paper or coloring medium. Cut out a large hole in tail or mouth end of fish for catching with opened paper clip hook. To operate: Put hand between the plates and move about the playing space.

Other sealife can be made from the basic puppet construction. For example: add pleated paper legs for a crab, long fabric ribbon streamers for a jellyfish, or head and feet for a turtle.

To Make Fishing Pole — Attach a string to a dowel or stick. Tie a large opened paper clip to the end of string for a hook. Small magnets may also be considered, and attached to Fish for easy catching.

Puppetizing: Pretend that the playing circle is a big Sea and let half the group swim around the Sea with their Sealife puppets. The rest of the children should try to catch the Sealife as the rhyme is recited, using their arms as fishing rods (without lines and hooks). Reverse roles and repeat the rhyme. The addition of background music or soap bubbles will enhance the underwater mood of this activity.

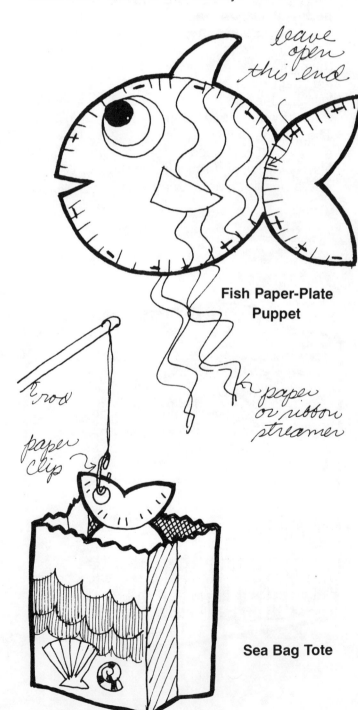

leave open this end

Fish Paper-Plate Puppet

rod

paper clip

paper or ribbon streamer

Sea Bag Tote

THIS IS THE WAY

This is the way the ladies ride,
Tri-tre-tre-tree,
Tri-tre-tre-tree!
This is the way the ladies ride,
Tri-tre-tre-tree, tri-tre-tre-tree!

This is the way the gentlemen ride,
Gallop-a-trot,
Gallop-a-trot!
This is the way the gentlemen ride,
Gallop-a-gallop-a-trot!

This is the way the farmers ride,
Hobbledy-hoy,
Hobbledy-hoy!
This is the way the farmers ride,
Hobbledy-hobbledy-hoy!

Introducing the Rhyme: Ask the children, "Have you ever ridden on a real horse?" "What did you like best about being on a horse?" "Do you know what it means when a horse gallops?" "Trots?"

Puppetelling: Recite the rhyme while holding a Horse Tube Puppet and bouncing the puppet along to different tempos.

Puppetmaking: Ask each child to make a Horse Tube Puppet to ride along with the rhyme.

Materials — Photocopy of two Horse's head patterns; cardboard towel tube; and yarn or fringed paper.

Construction — Cut out and color head patterns. Attach one head pattern to each side of the tube. Staple the lower face portion together for extra strength. Add a yarn or fringed paper mane to top of head.

Puppetizing: Pretend that the playing circle is a large circus ring and arrange the children outside the ring. Then, one at a time, call the children to enter the ring, riding their Horse puppets. You may wish to use each child's name in calling out special commands for the horse to perform in the ring. For example:

"This is the way that Mary _____."
(Trots, bumps, prances, bounces, runs, jumps, gallops, etc.)

Afterwards each child can think up a clever trick for the Horse to perform in the ring, such as standing on its head or jumping a hurdle.

fringed paper

tube

HORSE PATTERN

THREE LITTLE KITTENS

Mother: *My three little kittens*
Lost their mittens,
And they began to cry.

Kittens: *Oh, mother dear, we sadly fear,*
Our mittens we have lost.

Mother: *What! Lost your mittens,*
You naughty kittens!
Then you shall have no pie.

Kittens: *Mee-ow, mee-ow, mee-ow . . .*

Mother: *No, you shall have no pie.*

Mother: *My three little kittens*
Found their mittens,
And they began to cry.

Kittens: *Oh, mother dear, see here,*
see here,
Our mittens we have found.

Mother: *What! Found your mittens,*
You good little kittens!
Then you shall have some pie.

Kittens: *Purr-r, purr-r, purr-r . . .*

Mother: *Yes, you shall have some pie.*

Mother: *My three silly kittens*
Put on their mittens,
And soon ate up the pie.

Kittens: *Oh, mother dear, we*
greatly fear,
Our mittens we have soiled.

Mother: *What! Soiled your mittens,*
You naughty kittens!
Then they began to sigh.

Kittens: *Mee-ow, mee-ow, mee-ow . . .*

Mother: *Then they began to sigh.*

Mother: *My three little kittens*
Washed their mittens,
And hung them out to dry.

Kittens: *Oh, mother dear, look here,*
look here,
Our mittens we have washed.

Mother: *What! Washed your mittens,*
You darling kittens!
But I smell a rat close by.

Kittens: *Hush! Hush! Hush!*

Mother and
Kittens: *Yes, we smell a rat close by.*

Introducing the Rhyme: Ask the children, "Have you ever lost something you weren't supposed to?" "Did your mother or father get angry with you?" "What did you say?" "How did you feel when you found it again?"

Puppetelling: Wearing a Mother Cat Mask, pretend you are the Mother Cat and recite the poem while using contrasting character voices, preferably a lower voice for the Mother Cat and a higher voice to represent the Kittens. Let three children pantomime the Kittens' actions, without puppets, using real mittens as props.

Puppetmaking: Ask each child to make a Paper-Plate Kitten Mask to use with the rhyme.

Materials — Paper plate; string or large rubber band; construction paper; and yarn.

Construction — Cut out round eye holes and a triangle nose hole on the paper plate; add paper ears and yarn whiskers to complete the face. Punch small holes on sides of the mask to secure string or opened rubber band for attaching to head. Slip mask over face.

Puppetizing: Divide all the Kittens into groups of three and have each group think up something that they as Kittens have lost, such as shoes, hats, crayons, etc. Then recite the rhyme, repeatedly, letting each group play the Kittens while substituting their selected lost items into the rhyme. To simplify the activity, repeat only the first two verses for each group and let the group respond with appropriate dialogue.

Cat Paper-Plate Mask

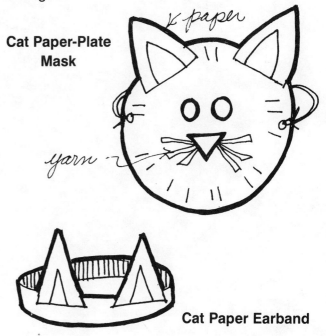

Cat Paper Earband

TWINKLE, TWINKLE, LITTLE STAR

Twinkle, twinkle, little star,
How I wonder what you are!
Up above the world so high,
Like a diamond in the sky.

When the blazing sun is gone,
When there's nothing to shine upon;
Then you show your little light,
Twinkle, twinkle, all the night.
When little children in the dark,
Thank you for your tiny spark!

Introducing the Rhyme: Ask the children, "At nighttime, what are all the different things you see as you look up at the sky?" "What color is the night sky?" "What color are the stars?" Talk about the word "twinkle" and what it means. "What are other things that sometimes twinkle?" (eyes, jewels, etc.)

Puppetelling: Recite the rhyme holding an Instant Star Puppet high above your head as if in the sky.

Puppetmaking: Ask the children to make their own Instant Star Puppets to twinkle in the sky.

Materials — Photocopy of pattern; and sticky-backed masking tape.

Construction — Cut out and color Star pattern. Put a piece of double-stick tape on back and secure to hand as shown. Move thumb and first finger apart to make puppet talk.

Puppetizing: Pretend the classroom is a big night sky. Ask the children to find a special place for their Star to "twinkle" in the sky. When they are in their positions, repeat the rhyme while they make their own stars twinkle. At the end of the activity, ask the children to close their eyes and pretend that their Star is the first star of the evening and make a wish. Each child's twinkling star can then share its wish with the group.

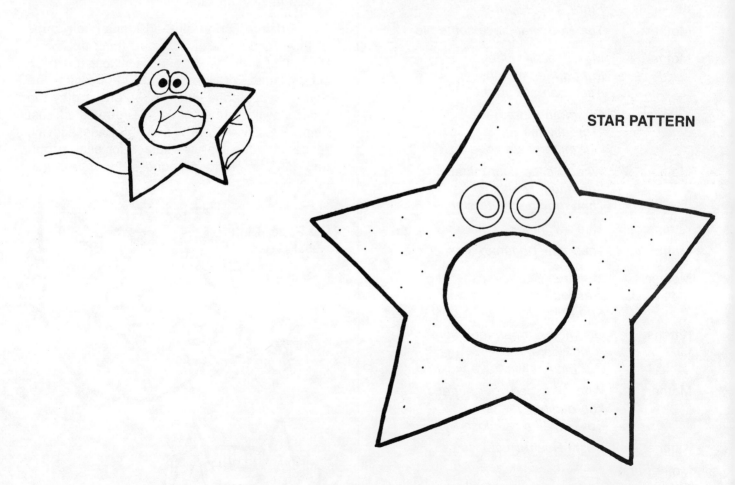

STAR PATTERN

TWO BIRDS

There were two birds sat on a stone,
Fa, la, la, la, lal, de;
One flew away, and then there was one,
Fa, la, la, la, lal, de.

The other bird flew after,
And then there was none,
Fa, la, la, la, lal, de;
And so the stone was left alone,
Fa, la, la, la, lal, de.

One of the birds then back again flew,
Fa, la, la, la, lal, de;
The other came after, and then there
* were two;*
Fa, la, la, la, lal, de.

Introducing the Rhyme: Ask the children, "What is your favorite bird?" "What color is it?" "What does it enjoy doing?" (sing, fly, catch worms, etc.) "Where do birds sometimes like to sit?" "If you were a bird, how would you sing?"

Puppetelling: Select a child to be the stone and form her body into a stone shape positioned directly in front of you. Recite the rhyme with the two Bird Stick Puppets flying away from the stone and hiding behind your back at the appropriate times.

Puppetmaking: Group the children into teams of two and have them create simple Stick Puppets of other sets of characters of their choosing, such as spiders, monkey, or snakes.

Materials — Construction paper; and drinking straw or blunt skewer for rod control.

Construction — Cut out character from construction paper and add features with paper or coloring medium. Attach character image to end of rod control.

Puppetizing: Choose someone to be the stone and invite each team to act out the rhyme while changing the words of the rhyme to match each set of characters. Instead of using the word "flew," consider other verbs to describe the new character's actions, such as Bugs—*crawl,* Grasshoppers—*hop,* Snakes—*slither,* Frogs—*leap,* and Leopards—*run.*

paper body

rod

NANCY RENFRO STUDIOS

Special Media for Mother Goose Fun

BOOKS In Paperback

Puppetry In Early Childhood Education by Tamara Hunt and Nancy Renfro. Comprehensive resource for "Puppetization" of hundreds of new learning activites, Preschool through Grade 3.

Puppetry and the Art of Story Creation by Nancy Renfro. Excellent guide on "how-to" create a story with many simple puppet ideas for an integrated curriculum approach. Special section on puppetry for the disabled.

A Puppet Corner In Every Library by Nancy Renfro. Superb step-by-step guide for incorporating puppetry into the library for storytelling, loan-bags and setting up a puppet corner.

Puppetry and Creative Dramatics in Storytelling by Connie Champlin, illustrated by Nancy Renfro. Imaginative puppetry and creative dramatics activities for group participation based on children's literature.

Make Amazing Puppets by Nancy Renfro and Beverly Armstrong. Jammed packed with exciting ideas for making puppets from paper products and recycled junk.

Books, Puppets And The Mentally Retarded Student by John and Connie Champlin, illustrated by Carol A. Anderson. How to select and adapt books for telling stories; techniques for utilizing puppetry in programs.

An Exciting Series:

Pocketful of Puppets: Activities for the Special Child by Debbie Sullivan, illustrated by Nancy Renfro

Pocketful of Puppets: Mother Goose Rhymes by Tamara Hunt and Nancy Renfro

Pocketful of Puppets: Three Plump Fish and Other Short Stories by Yvonne Winer, illustrated by Nancy Renfro

Pocketful of Puppets: Poems for Church School by Lynn Irving, illustrated by Nancy Renfro

WRITE FOR FREE CATALOGUE:
Over 200 Puppet Characters • Show Kits • Books

Nancy Renfro Studios
1117 W. 9th Street, Austin, Tx 78703
(512) 472-2140